Handmade
Gifts

Handmade Gifts

DK

LONDON, NEW YORK,
MELBOURNE, MUNICH, and DELHI

DK UK
Project Art Editor Gemma Fletcher
Project Editor Laura Palosuo
Designer Charlotte Johnson
Jacket Designer Rosie Levine
Pre-Production Producer Rebecca Fallowfield
Producer Ché Creasey
Photographer Dave King
Creative Technical Support Sonia Charbonnier
Managing Editor Penny Smith
Managing Art Editor Marianne Markham
Art Director Jane Bu
Publisher Mary Lin

DK INDIA
Senior Art Editor Ivy
Art Editor Vikas Sachc
Assistant Art Editor Pallav
Managing Art Editor Navid
Pre-Production Manager Su
Production Manager Panka
Senior DTP Designer Jagt
DTP Designers Syed Md
Rajesh Singh Adhikari, Rajd

First published in Great Britain in 2013
by Dorling Kindersley Limited,
80 Strand, London, WC2R 0RL

2 4 6 8 10 9 7 5 3 1

192398 – Aug/2013

A CIP catalogue record for this book
Is available from the British Library

ISBN 978-1-4093-3405-7
Printed and bound by South China in China

Discover more at
www.dk.com

Contents

Introduction

Sometimes a box of chocolates or another pair of socks simply won't do. For a truly thoughtful present, making your own gifts is the way forward: you can create something beautiful, unique, and affordable, regardless of whether you have an hour or two to spend or an afternoon.

Every idea in *Handmade Gifts* is explained in step-by-step photographs so you can be sure that your gift will have a professional finish, and will be well worth the time you invest. If the project needs a template, we include one so you know it will work. There are lots of ideas for how you can add your own twist, so you can make the gift that is exactly right for the person you have in mind.

We have included a range of gift ideas, each requiring different levels of skill and time – for example, you can crochet a beaded necklace or "cheat" with a knotted one. We hope you have a wonderful time making your gifts... and that you find time to make something for yourself!

For the home

Customized
cushion

Customize a plain cushion cover with appliqué fabric shapes, buttons, and decorative stitches to make a stylish or funky cushion at a low cost – a perfect gift for a new home or for a child's bedroom.

To make a blossom cushion you will need

Tools: washable ink pen • tracing paper • steam iron • dressmaker's scissors • sewing pins • sewing machine • sewing needle • cotton sewing threads *Materials:* iron-on interfacing • brown cotton fabric • white cotton fabric • pink floral cotton fabric • green felt • cushion cover • 8 small white buttons and 4 large white buttons

 1

Enlarge the blossom cushion templates on p.226 to fit your cushion. Trace all the shapes apart from the leaves onto iron-on interfacing.

 2

Cut out the interfacing and iron each piece onto the chosen fabric for each: brown cotton for the bird and branch, white cotton for 12 petals, and pink floral cotton for 12 centres.

3

Carefully cut out all
the interfaced shapes.

4

Trace the leaf template onto paper and cut it out.
Use the template to trace and cut out six leaves
from the felt. There is no need to iron these onto
interfacing as felt will not fray.

6

Machine sew the branch and bird onto
the cushion using a contrasting colour
cotton thread, carefully sewing about
3–5mm (¹/₈–¼in) from the edges.

7

Match the large, white flowers with the large,
pink centres and the small, white flowers with
the small, pink centres. Place the flowers and
leaves onto the cushion and pin in position.

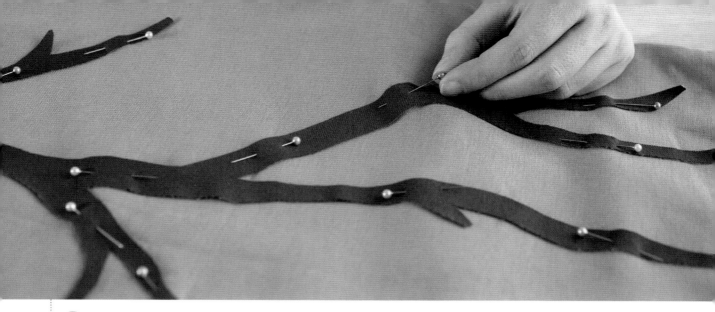

 5

Place the cushion cover on a flat surface and place the branch and bird in position. Pin or use tacking stitches to secure.

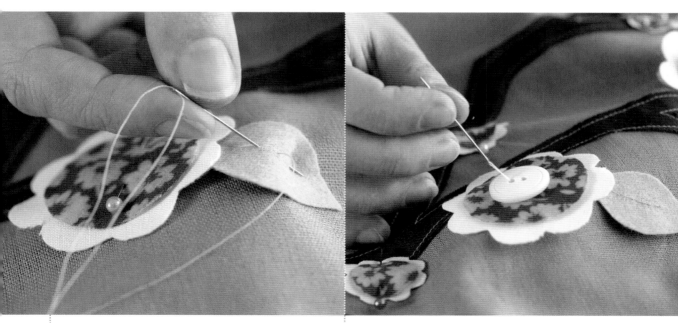

 8

Tuck some of the leaves behind the flowers to create a natural effect. Hand sew the leaves on in a matching cotton down the centres, using four or five backstitches to secure.

 9

Sew large and small buttons into the centres of the flowers, sewing through the cushion cover to secure the flowers to the cover.

Castle cushion

Be as creative as you like with this castle.
Start with the template on p.228 to create
the basic shape. Use leather-effect fabric for
the drawbridge and windows, and a favourite
colour for the flag. The prince and princess are
made from felt offcuts and are attached to the
cushion by thin cord so they cannot be lost!
You can make your own, or add ready-made
fabric dolls. Remember to make a few pockets
in the design for them to go into.

*Tip: Use the templates
on p.229 to make the dolls.
Add yarn for hair and
sew or draw the faces.*

Skull and crossbones cushion

A fun skull motif will appeal to children of all ages, particularly those with a love of pirates! Find the template for this project on p.227. Cut out the skull and crossbone shapes from black felt and tack into position on the cushion cover. Machine sew around the edge of the black shapes using white cotton. Cut out eyes and teeth from white felt and sew them by hand into position, onto the skull.

Guitar cushion

This is the perfect cushion for a teenager's room. Using the template on p.227, cut out the shapes for the guitar from black and white felt or suede-effect fabric. Tack and stitch the guitar body into place first, using contrast thread. Add the white board section, sewing it on with white thread. Add the black details, again using contrast thread. Use white ribbon for the strings, and stitch into position. A drum or a section of piano keys would also look effective.

Personalized journal

For the home

What better place to store notes and thoughts than in a handmade journal with a personalized cover? This technique demands precision – each stage leads on to the next, so if you're slightly "out", the journal may look misshapen.

To make a journal you will need

Tools: bone folder • craft knife • pencil • metal ruler • self-healing cutting mat • sewing needle
Materials: 6 sheets of heavy A3 white or cream paper • 1 sheet of A3 decorative paper • white thread

1
Making sure that the grain is running vertically, fold each piece of white or cream A3 paper in half so that the short edges meet. Smooth the crease with the bone folder.

2
Starting from the inside of the folded sheet, cut along the fold with the knife, stopping at a point just over halfway along the fold.

3

Fold each sheet of paper in half again, short edge to short edge. Crease then cut along the fold, stopping just after halfway. Fold the paper in half again, short edge to short edge, and crease.

4

Assemble the folded sheets in a pile of "stacks". To make the cover, first fold the decorative paper in half so that the long edges meet and press the crease down with the bone folder.

7

Use the ruler and the bone folder to crease the cover along the second pencil line you have just drawn. The area between the two creases will be the spine of your journal.

8

Measure the height of the cover, and divide this distance into five equal sections. Mark each section on the spine, and then use a craft knife to cut a slit through each line.

5

Fold the paper in half again, this time so that the short edges meet. Smooth down the crease with the bone folder.

6

Open the cover and draw a line down the crease. Press down gently on the pile of stacks and measure the height of the pile. Then measure the same distance to one side of the crease. Draw a line.

9

Use the ruler to draw lines on the pile of paper stacks to correspond with the slits in the cover.

10

Open up each paper segment and prick the needle through each mark. There should now be four evenly spaced holes in each paper segment. Thread the needle.

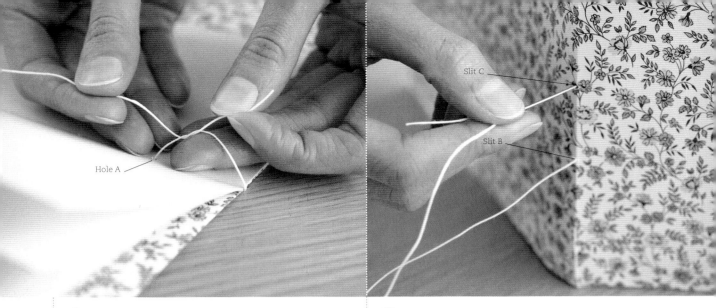

11

With one stack on top of the cover, push the needle through the first hole (hole A) and first slit (slit A) from the inside. Pass the thread around the top of the spine and tie a knot.

12

Pass the needle through the hole B from the inside and out through slit B. Run the thread along the spine and push the needle in through slit C and hole C to the inside.

15

Add a new stack and continue, securing pages and adding stacks. After the last stack, pass the needle around the top of the journal, and below one of the stitches. Knot on the inside.

16

Fold the decorative paper back over the stack and smooth it down, creasing the fold with your finger.

13

Push the needle out through hole D and slit D. Looping the thread around the bottom of the spine, push the needle through just hole D again. Tighten the thread.

14

Add the next stack. Go through the first hole of the new stack (hole 2D) to the inside, then around the bottom of the spine and back through slit D and hole 2D. Continue, securing the second stack like the first.

17

Now fold the paper under again to form the jacket. Repeat for the other side.

18

Cut through the edges of the pages of the first stack. Repeat for all the other stacks.

Dot-decorated
ceramics

For the home

Painting ceramics by hand can seem a bit daunting, but this dot-decorating method is virtually foolproof. Almost any line-drawing can be turned into a dot painting, so once you have mastered the technique try out your own designs.

To make a dot-decorated vase you will need

Tools: scissors • ballpoint pen

Materials: ceramic vase • baby wipes or damp cloth • red transfer paper
• masking tape • black, food-safe ceramic pen or paint in a dispenser

1

Clean the vase to remove any loose dust or grease from the surface. Photocopy the vase template (see p.240) and reduce or enlarge it to fit.

2

Place a sheet of transfer paper behind the template and cut out the main dandelion motif. Then cut out the individual seeds.

27

3

Tape the dandelion template to the front of your vase, with the transfer paper underneath. Position the seeds around the template and on one adjoining side.

4

Using a ballpoint pen, firmly trace the design onto the vase. Use solid lines across the dots as these show up best.

7

Using the template as a guide, complete the design with dots. Keep the spacing of the dots even and work quickly to avoid the paint pooling. Paint short, solid lines at the ends of the seeds and then fill in the dots.

5

Remove the template and check that the lines are visible. If not, wipe away the trace lines and repeat the process, pressing down more firmly.

6

Use a ceramic paint pen or paint in a dispenser to draw the stem of the dandelion in one continuous line.

8

Repeat Steps 4–7 to decorate the second side of the vase. Let the paint dry before repeating the whole process for the remaining two sides.

9

When the paint is completely dry, use a baby wipe or damp cloth to wipe off the trace lines. Follow the paint manufacturer's instructions to set the paint.

Mug and coaster set

Create this delicately patterned mug and coaster set in exactly the same way as the vase (see pp.26–29) using the mug and coaster template (see p.241). When painting the dots, remember to work from left to right (right to left if you're left-handed) across the pattern to avoid smudging the dots you have already made.

Tip: Create a set of mugs using the same design in different colours — one for each family member.

Celebration bunting plate

As a rule, it is not safe to eat food from hand-painted ceramics (but do check the label on your paints). The dot-decorating method can be used to create stunning display plates though, and this bunting plate is the perfect gift to mark a celebration. Use the template (see p.241) to transfer the pattern to the plate. Draw the black lines, let them dry, then work across the pattern filling in the flags with coloured dots.

Tip: Add a celebratory message or the recipient's name to the plate by painting a letter in each flag.

Mosaic
bowl

This calming, woodland-inspired mosaic bowl is created using the direct method, meaning that tiles are glued straight onto the object and then grouted. This will not produce a completely level surface, resulting in a tactile bowl.

To make a mosaic bowl you will need

Tools: tile nippers • rubber gloves • protective mask & goggles • grout spreader • sponge • lint-free cloth

Materials: wooden bowl • tesserae in different shades of green • flat-backed beads and 5mm millefiori • PVA glue • mosaic grout (either pre-mixed or made up following the manufacturer's instructions)

1
Draw a wavy line onto your bowl, about 4.5cm (1¾in) from the rim. Draw a second line roughly 1.5cm (⅝in) below this one. This will be the first accent line on your bowl.

2
Prepare your tiles by soaking or peeling off any backing sheets. Select the plain tiles and those for the accent lines, and place them in groups of the same colour and type.

3

Cut tiles for the accent lines. Wearing goggles, hold the tile between thumb and forefinger and, positioning nippers at the edge, gently squeeze. Repeat to cut into quarters.

4

Arrange the tiles and embellishments between your wavy lines. Vary iridescent and matt tiles, as well as round and rectangular ones to create a pattern.

7

Complete one line at a time, increasing or decreasing the shade and adding accent lines at regular intervals. When complete, leave to dry overnight.

8

Wearing rubber gloves and a mask, apply the grout generously to the mosaic, working in different directions. Make sure to also grout around the outer edge of the bowl.

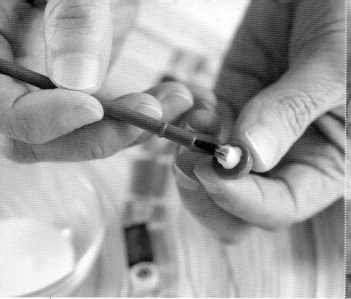
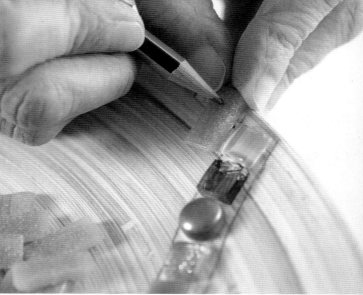

 5

Move the pieces off the line, keeping their order. Add a dab of glue to the back of each piece and stick them to your bowl leaving even gaps between them.

 6

For the lines of plain tiles, start with the lightest green tiles, and cut them in half (see Step 3). Glue them either side of the accent line, trimming them if necessary.

9

Use a damp sponge to carefully wipe away the excess grout. Leave for 20 minutes, then, before the grout is hard, wipe gently again.

 10

When the grout is completely dry, use a lint-free dry cloth to wipe away any residue and polish the tiles to a shine.

Owl jewellery box

You will need
Wooden box
Glazed and unglazed ceramic tiles
Glass nuggets and beads
White grout
Felt for base

This pretty jewellery box is made using the same technique as the mosaic bowl on pp.33–35. Start by drawing the design on the box (see template p.238) and then seal the box with watered-down PVA glue. Start filling in the design, attaching the nuggets and whole tiles first. Cut the remaining tiles to size to complete the design. Finally, fill in the area around the design with randomly cut tiles – a technique known as crazy paving. Allow to dry and then grout the lid. Grout the box one side at a time, waiting for each side to dry before starting the next. Glue felt to the base to finish the box.

Flower garland mirror

You will need
Mirror with wide, flat, wooden frame
A selection of tiles and glass nuggets
White grout

Make this mirror in the same way as the mosaic bowl on pp.33–35. Draw on the design first (see template p.239) and seal the wooden frame with watered-down PVA glue if necessary. Create the flowers first, starting with a nugget and using tile nippers to shape the petals. Next, make the leaf garlands. Fill in the gaps with crazy paving (see above), and use tile halves to fill in the outer edge of the border. Cover the mirror with masking tape to protect it when grouting. Grout the frame, ensuring you create a straight edge around the mirror.

Round tea light holder

You will need
Ball-shaped, wooden tea light holder
Old crockery, broken into small pieces
Tiles and glass nuggets
White grout
Felt for the base

This tea light holder is made in the same way as the mosaic bowl (see pp.33–35), but using fragments of broken crockery. First, draw your design (see p.239) on the tea light holder and then seal it with watered-down PVA glue. Glue down the nuggets first, and then use tile nippers to shape the crockery pieces into petals. Next, add any whole tiles. Finally, fill in the area around the design with more crockery pieces. Work a small area at a time. Some tiles may have to be held in place using tape until they dry. Grout, allow to dry, and attach felt to the base to finish.

Seaside coasters

You will need
MDF squares
Tiles in a variety of colours
Grey grout

These seaside-inspired coasters have been made out of squares of MDF, using the technique described for the mosaic bowl on pp.33–35. Using either the template from p.238 or your own design, first draw guidelines onto the coaster in pencil. Fill in the design first, shaping the tiles to fit. Try to keep the tiles fairly flat, as you will need to be able to rest a glass or mug on the coaster when finished. Next, fill in the background using square tiles, shaping them to fit as necessary. Again, try to keep the tiles as flat as possible. Grout the coasters, not forgetting the edges, to finish.

Ribbon-bound photo album

This wonderful album is bound to become a family treasure. Use thick, acid-free card for the pages to protect your photographs and thick, good-quality ribbon to ensure that the binding holds for years to come.

To make a ribbon-bound photo album you will need

Tools: craft knife • metal ruler • self-healing cutting mat • bookbinding needle

Materials: sheets of heavy white or cream paper • 3 x 15cm (5⅞in) lengths of ribbon • masking tape • 3 x 1m (40in) linen bookbinding thread • 2 sheets 2–3mm (¹⁄₁₆–⅛in) cardboard • 2 sheets decorative paper • glue • greaseproof paper

1
Find the grain of the paper by folding it over lengthways and widthways. The fold with least resistance tells you that the grain runs up and down.

2
With the grain running vertically, use the template (see p.236) to cut 18 rectangles to make 15 pages, two end papers, and one sewing template.

3

Transfer the hole markings to one sheet to use as your sewing template. One at a time, line up each of the 15 pages with the sewing template and pierce the needle through each mark.

4

Place one page at the edge of a table, the pierced side lined up with the table edge. Position the three lengths of ribbon between each set of holes, and tape them to the edge of the table.

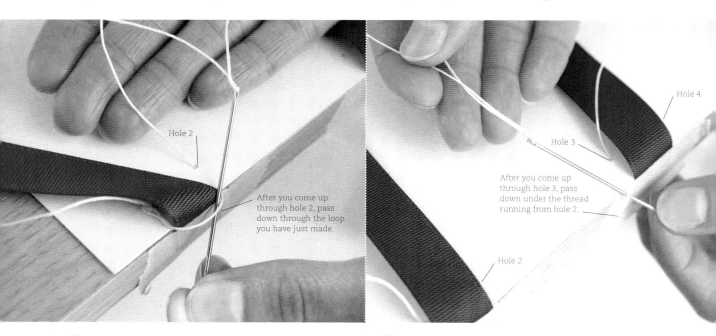

Hole 2

After you come up through hole 2, pass down through the loop you have just made.

Hole 4

Hole 3

After you come up through hole 3, pass down under the thread running from hole 2.

Hole 2

7

After you come up through the second hole, flip the ribbons over the paper. Pass down through the loop you have just made. Take care not to pull too tight, keeping all the loops slightly loose.

8

Next pass through hole 3, bottom to top, then under the thread running from hole 2. Pass through hole 4, bottom to top, and through the loop you have just made (see Step 7).

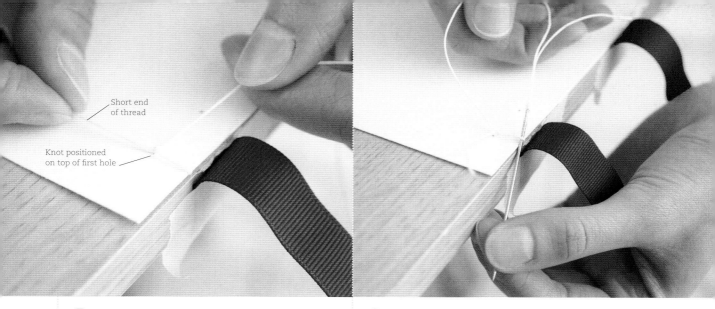

5

Flip the ribbons off the paper. Using a needle and 1m (40in) thread, go through the first hole from top to bottom. Loop around and tie a double knot, positioning it on top of the hole.

6

Pass the needle underneath the loop you have just made, right to left, and pull the thread through. Pass under the ribbon, and through the second hole, going from underneath to top.

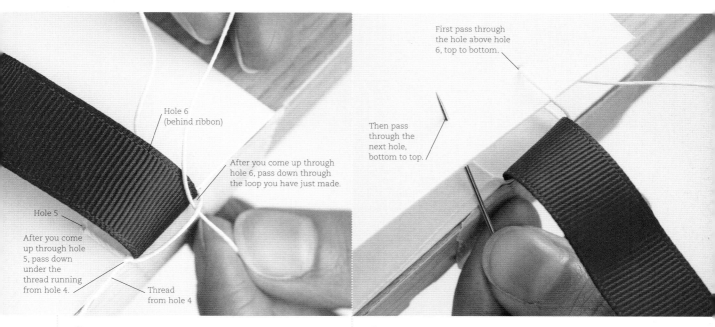

9

Repeat for holes 5 and 6: pass up through hole 5, bottom to top, and under the thread running from hole 4; pass up through hole 6, and down through the loop.

10

Add the second page. Pass through the hole above hole 6, top to bottom, across the ribbon, and come up through the next hole. Repeat Steps 7–9 in reverse, but don't go through the last loop.

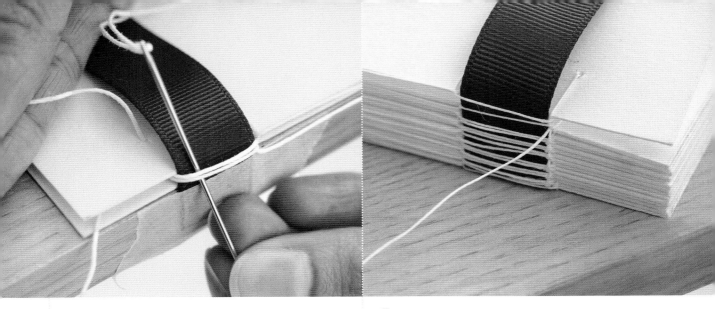

11

After you come up through the last hole on the second page, pass down through the last loop as well as the loop below it. Add the next page, and pass through the first two holes as in Step 10.

12

Repeat Steps 7–11 for the remaining 13 pages, always passing through both the last loop and the loop below it, securing the loops together in bunches of two. When you run out of thread, attach more with a weaver's knot.

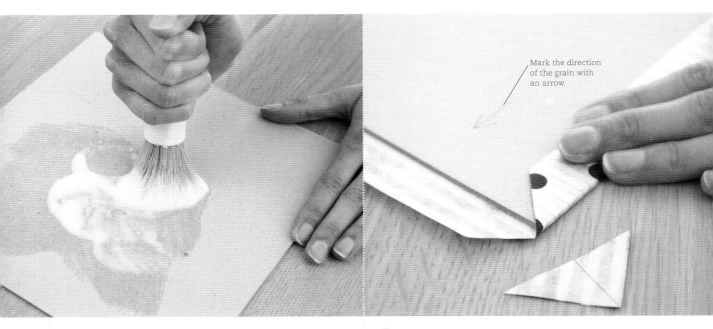

Mark the direction of the grain with an arrow.

14

Cut two cardboard covers, 3mm (⅛in) longer than the pages at the top, bottom, and one side. Cut two sheets of decorative paper, 2cm (¾in) longer on all sides than the boards. Spread glue on each board.

15

With the grain running vertically, place each board, glue side down, in the centre of one sheet of paper. Trim each corner diagonally and glue the edges over the board.

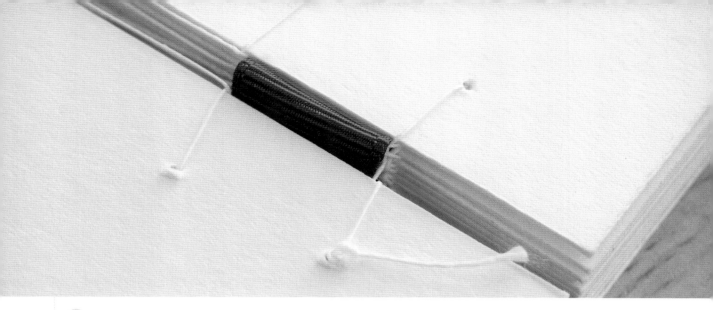

13

With the book closed, push the needle underneath the first page. Open the first page and pull the thread through. Next, push the needle through the first hole on the second page. Turn the page, pull the thread through, and tie a knot on the other side of the second page. Cut the thread.

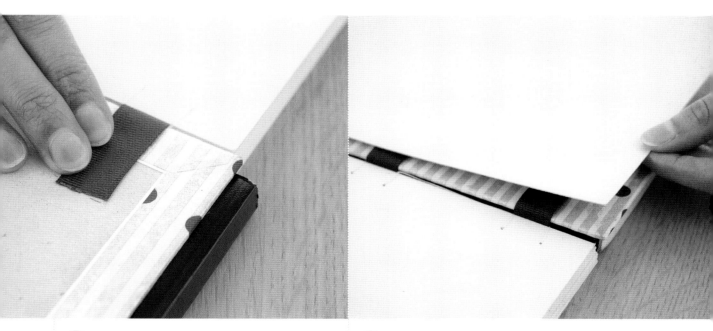

16

Place one cover on a book the same height as the stack of pages to hold it level and glue down the ribbon ends. Repeat for the other cover, trimming the ribbons if needed.

17

Glue the endpapers to the insides of each board to conceal the ribbons. Place greaseproof paper between both covers and first pages. Weigh down the album and let it dry overnight.

Photo album variation

Once you have mastered the binding
technique explained on pp.39–43, you can
create endless variations of the album for
different purposes and recipients. The
nostalgic feel of this vintage-inspired album
makes it the perfect place to store heirloom
photographs. Cut the pages and covers in a
landscape shape and use two sets of narrow
ribbons to work the stitching around. Instead
of sandwiching the ribbons between the
covers and endpapers, glue them to the
outside of the covers to create a look
reminiscent of antique book bindings.

*Tip: Vary the colours
of the pages, too — pink
or blue for baby albums
and black for black-and-
white photographs.*

Rollaway gameboard

This draughts board has an integrated pocket for game pieces and it rolls up neatly, making it easy to store and ideal for travel. The patchwork top is cleverly made from fabric strips, saving you having to piece each square separately.

To make a rollaway gameboard you will need

Tools: dressmaker's scissors • sewing machine • sewing pins • iron

Materials: plain fabric in brown and cream • decorative fabric in two different designs • cotton sewing thread • interfacing • 3cm (1⅛in) button • thin ribbon • buttons in 2 colours to use as draught pieces

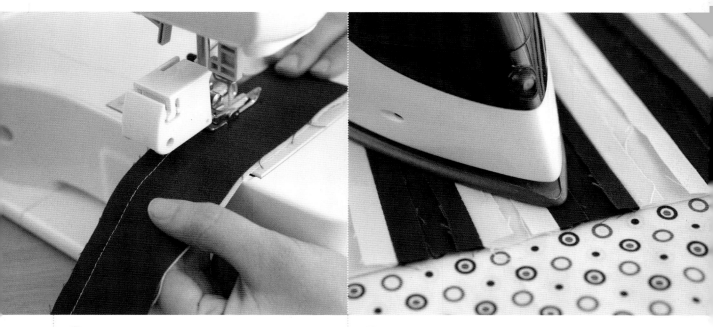

1

Use the chart in the Templates section (p.229) to measure and cut out the fabric pieces. Sew together one light and one dark strip with a 1cm (⅜in) seam allowance.

2

Sew a light strip to the other edge of the first dark strip. Add the remaining strips one at a time, alternating colours. Press all the seams open, forming a 29cm (12in) wide piece.

3

Mark lines across the strips every 5cm (2in). Cut along the lines to make eight bands. Pin the bands together, offsetting every other row by one square to make a chequerboard.

4

Sew the strips together with a 1cm (⅜in) seam allowance. Press open the seams. Trim off the extra squares on either side to create an 8 x 8 board, leaving the seam allowance.

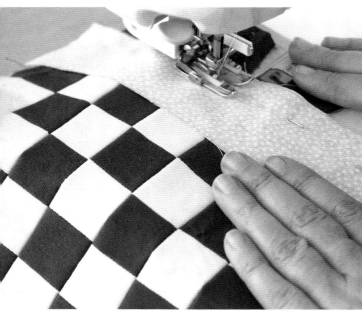

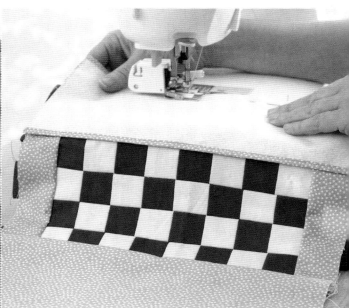

7

Place the two narrow strips of inner fabric at two opposite sides of the board, right side to right side. Pin, then sew with a 1cm (⅜in) seam allowance. Press the seams open.

8

Sew the two remaining inner fabric panels to the two remaining edges of the board with a 1cm (⅜in) seam allowance. Press the seams away from the board.

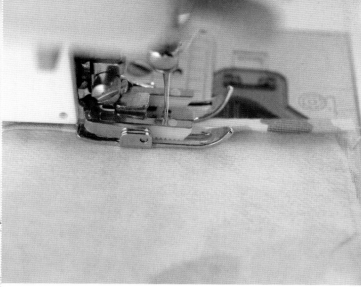

5

Apply interfacing to the wrong side of the 30 x 50cm (12 x 20in) piece of outer fabric and one of the 30 x 14cm (12 x 5¾in) pieces of inner fabric.

6

Fold over a 5mm (¼in) double hem at one end of the interfaced outer fabric and stitch. Do the same along one long edge of the interfaced inner fabric. These will form the pocket edges.

9

Place the right side of the outer fabric and the right side of the inner fabric together, making sure the pocket hems (see step 6) line up. Pin, then sew with 1cm (⅜in) seam allowance along three sides, leaving the pocket edges open.

10

Overstitch along the edge of the chequerboard closest to the pocket edges to form an interlined pocket. You can use the pocket to store the game pieces.

11

Sew a 3cm (1¼in) button in the middle of the outside of the non-pocket end, approximately 1.5cm (⅝in) from the edge. Thread a thin ribbon through the buttonhole.

12

Tie a knot in the ribbon behind the button. Wrap the ribbon around the rolled-up game, securing the counters inside. Secure the roll by winding the ribbon around the button.

Jewellery

Beaded
necklace

There is such a wealth of beautiful beads to choose from, including ceramic, glass, enamel, and hand-painted. Design a unique piece of jewellery using this simple and versatile knot technique.

To make a beaded necklace you will need
Tools: scissors
Materials: reel of 1mm-wide, black, waxed cotton thread
• 5 large beads • 6 small beads

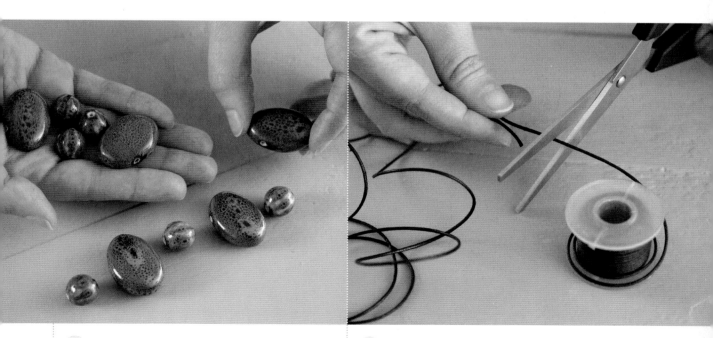

1
Choose beads with holes that are large enough to thread onto the waxed cotton thread. Plan out the order of your beads, and lay them in order on the work surface.

2
Cut two lengths of waxed cotton thread roughly twice the length you want the necklace to be. You could tie the thread around your neck first to judge the length.

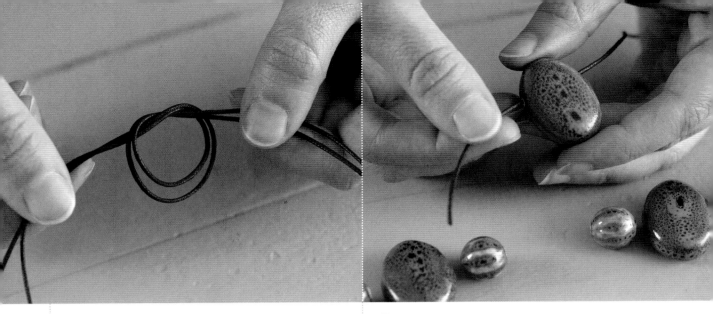

3

Lay the two strands of waxed cotton thread together. Fold the strands in half and tie a knot at this mid-point. This doesn't need to be very accurate, as the threads will be trimmed later.

4

Take the middle bead from your design and thread it onto one of the strands from either side. Slide it down until it reaches the first knot.

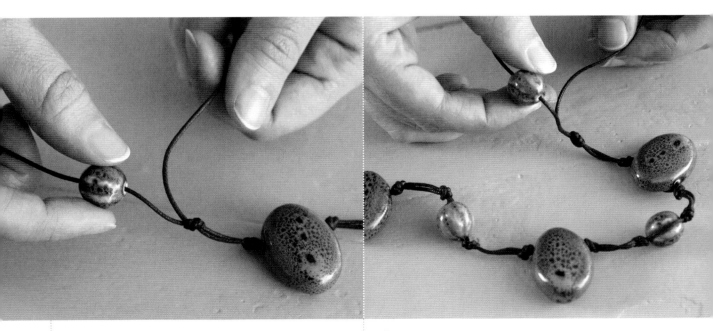

7

Take the next bead in your design and thread onto one strand. Again, pass the other strand behind the bead, then take both strands and tie a knot to secure the bead in position.

8

Take the next bead from your design and thread and knot as before, leaving a 2cm (¾in) gap each time. Repeat until you have finished one side of the necklace, then thread and knot the other side.

5

Pass the other strand behind the bead and tie both strands together in a knot on the other side of the bead to secure the bead in position.

6

Leave a gap of approximately 2cm (¾in), and tie another knot with both threads together.

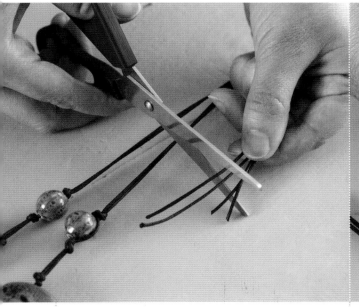

9

When you have threaded on your final bead, secure it with a knot. Place the ends of the necklace alongside each other and cut the strands of thread to the same length.

10

Knot one end of the necklace around the other end. Then knot the remaining loose end around the other end. You can now adjust the length of the necklace by sliding the knots.

Colour variation

Once you have mastered the technique on pp.55–57, you can experiment with different bead colours and sizes. Keeping colours within the same palette works well, and you can introduce different sizes without your necklace becoming fussy.

Tip: Opaque and tinted beads from the same colour palette work well together.

Painted beads

Hand-painted beads are expensive but making your own jewellery is a cost-effective way to showcase just a few hand-picked beautiful beads. If using beads with a varied pattern, keep the size the same.

Tip: Use coloured waxed cotton thread to match or contrast with your beads and help colours stand out.

Button-bead necklace

Flat button beads work well knotted together. This design knots the beads closely for a more formal look.

1   Tie a knot. Thread each strand through a bead as if sewing a button, passing through the bead from opposite sides.

2   Pull both strands tight, and tie a knot to secure. Repeat with the next bead, tying them close.

Tip: The knotting technique also works for flat or unusual-shaped beads.

Make all of these pretty brooches in exactly the same way as the bird brooch on pp.61–63. Templates for the other shapes are given on p.237.

Embellished
felt brooches

It's hard to believe that scraps of fabric and felt, buttons, ribbon, and beads are all that are needed to make these whimsical brooches. Turn a brooch into a key ring or bag charm by attaching a split ring to the top with a ribbon.

To make a bird brooch you will need

Tools: pencil • dressmaker's scissors • iron • damp cloth *Materials:* double-sided bonding web • patterned fabric • 3 squares of felt in contrasting colours • 1 skein of stranded cotton embroidery thread • extra-heavy-weight sew-in interfacing • 35 seed beads • 1 black bead • 15cm (6in) narrow ribbon • 1 small button • cotton sewing thread • brooch pin

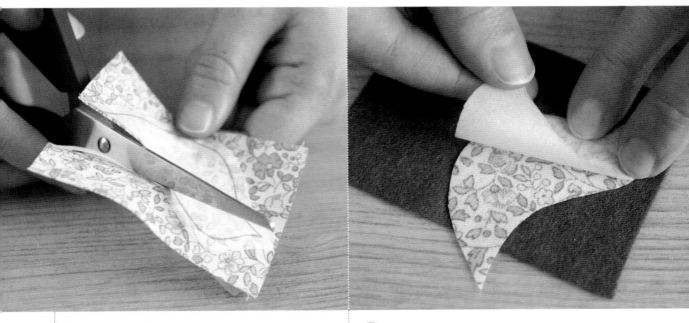

1 Trace the bird template on p.237 onto the paper side of the bonding web. Cut around the bird and iron it, textured side down, onto the reverse of the patterned fabric. Cut out the bird.

2 Peel off the backing paper. Place the bird face side up on the first felt square. Cover with a damp cloth and iron for a few seconds until the bird is bonded to the felt.

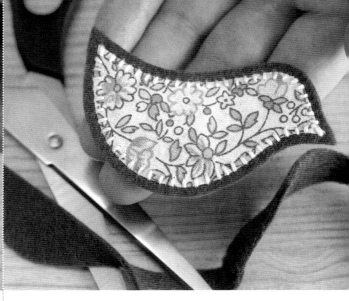

Using three strands of the cotton embroidery thread, stitch around the bird shape using an overstitch.

Cut the felt around the bird, leaving a felt border of approximately 3–5mm (⅛–¼in).

Using the wing template on p.237, cut a wing out of the first colour of felt. Stitch the wing onto the bird with the embroidery thread using a small running stitch.

8

Stitch on the black bead for the eye. Cut the ribbon in half and sew on two small ribbon loops for the tail. Using the embroidery thread, sew on the button to cover the ends of the ribbon.

5

Place the bird onto the contrasting shade of felt with the interfacing underneath. Using sewing cotton, sew on the seed beads, sewing through all three layers.

6

Carefully cut around the bird shape, again leaving a border of approximately 3–5mm (⅛–¼in). Make sure that you cut through both the contrasting felt and the interfacing.

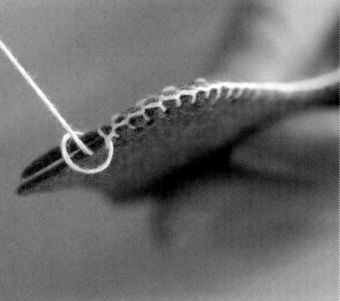

9

Using the brooch as a guide, cut an identical shape out of the last colour of felt to use as the backing. Using the embroidery thread, attach the backing with blanket stitch.

10

Using doubled sewing thread for strength, stitch the brooch pin on the reverse side of the brooch. Ensure you only stitch through the backing felt.

Silver clay
jewellery

Make beautiful silver jewellery items easily with silver clay. Available from craft shops, silver clay is 99% silver. When fired with a kitchen torch, the clay burns off, leaving behind a fully silver item.

For a silver leaf pendant you will need

Tools: Teflon mat or greaseproof paper • small rolling pin or piece of pipe • playing cards • craft knife • small straw • wet and dry sandpaper (600 grit) or sanding pad (220 grit) • kitchen blowtorch • firing brick or ceramic tile • timer • tweezers • soft wire brush • 2 pairs of pliers *Materials:* oil (cooking spray is ideal) • 7g (¼oz) silver clay • real leaves or leaf skeletons • silver jump ring

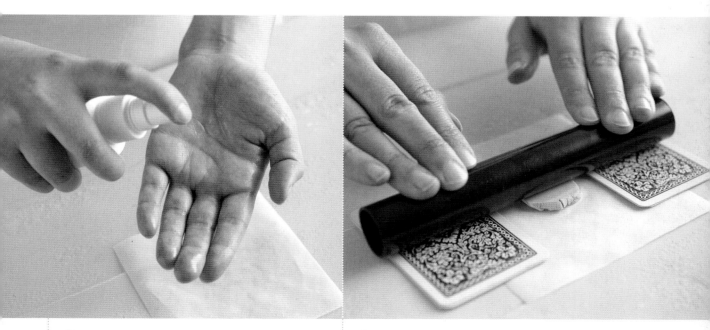

1
Cut out a square of greaseproof paper or use a Teflon mat. Prepare your work surface by rubbing a small amount of oil over the paper or mat, your hands, and the rolling pin.

2
Place two stacks of four playing cards each about 5cm (2in) away from each other to act as rolling guides. Soften the clay in your hands and roll it flat.

3

Lift up the rolled clay carefully and place a leaf underneath and on top of it as shown, ensuring you line up the stems and tips of the leaves. Roll over the clay again to imprint both sides.

4

Carefully remove the leaves, and lay the clay on a cutting mat or chopping board. Using the craft knife and the template from p.237, carefully cut a leaf shape from the clay.

7

Place the leaf on the firing brick or tile in a dimly lit, well-ventilated room. Hold the torch 5cm (2in) from the clay and move the flame evenly over it. The leaf will start to glow a peachy orange colour.

8

Once the leaf begins to glow, set the timer for two minutes. If the leaf turns bright red or shiny silver, it is too hot – move the flame away. Once fired, pick up the leaf with tweezers and quench it in water.

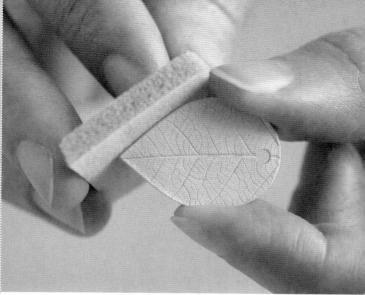

5

Using the straw, make a hole in the leaf about 5mm (¼in) from the top. This needs to be big enough for your jump ring, bearing in mind that the clay may shrink by up to 10% when fired.

6

Leave the clay to dry overnight, or to speed up the process use a hairdryer or put the clay in an oven at 150°C (300°F/Gas 2) for 10 minutes. Once dry, sand it very carefully to smooth the edges.

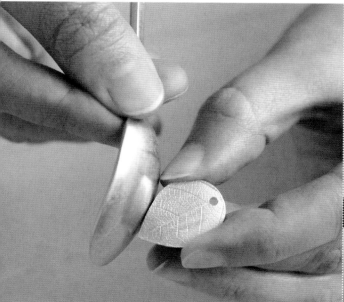

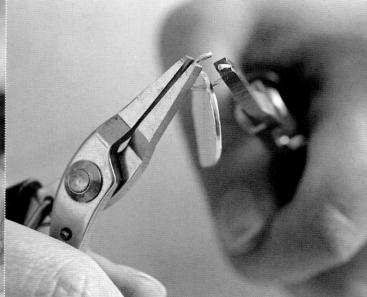

9

The leaf will now be a matt-white colour, even though it is pure silver. Gently brush it with a soft wire brush to reveal the silver colour. To achieve a high shine, rub with the back of a metal spoon.

10

Using two pairs of pliers, gently twist the ends of the jump ring away from each other. Thread it through the hole in your leaf, and then twist the jump ring closed.

Simple button cufflinks

A huge array of textured paper is available from most craft shops; a snakeskin pattern has been used to create these cufflinks made using the same technique as the silver leaf pendant on pp.65–67 and the cufflink templates on p.237. To make, roll out and texture approximately 20g (¾oz) of silver clay. Carefully cut out two discs measuring 2cm (¾in) in diameter, and another two of 1.5cm (⅝in) in diameter. Pierce each of these discs twice using a cocktail stick (the holes should be positioned to resemble the holes in a button). Dry out and fire the clay as for the silver leaf pendant. Burnish for a high shine, then using a needle and silver thread stitch the silver clay buttons onto a cufflink chain: 1.5–2cm (⅝–¾in) of chain with roughly 5mm (¼in) links is ideal. Tie off the thread, and use a tiny dot of superglue to ensure the end doesn't come loose.

Wallpaper earrings

Patterned wallpaper can be ideal for texturing metal clays, and the variety of designs available is huge. Make these earrings using the same technique as for the silver leaf pendant on pp.65–67, using 15g (½oz) of silver clay. Using the wallpaper, roll and texture your clay as before. Cut ovals from the clay approximately 3cm (1¼in) in length using the template on p.237, and pierce at the top with your straw. Dry out, and torch fire. Burnish for a high shine, and attach ear wires.

Leaf bracelet

This simple leaf bracelet requires approximately 25g (1oz) of silver clay. Roll and texture your clay as for the silver leaf pendant on pp.65–67. Then cut out seven pointed ellipses 2.5cm (1in) in length. Pierce each end of the ellipses with your straw. While the pieces of clay are still soft lay them over a rolling pin to give them a curved shape. Leave them to dry, and then torch fire as before. Link the elements together using jump rings, and finally attach a simple clasp.

Lace heart key ring

Fabrics, in particular lace, can be used to produce beautifully delicate patterns in metal clays. To make this heart key ring in the same way as the silver leaf pendant on pp.65–67, roll out approximately 10g (⅜oz) of silver clay. Texture it using lace, and then cut out a heart shape 3.5cm (1⅜in) in length using the template on p.237. Pierce the top of the heart with your straw. Dry out and fire the clay, then burnish to a high shine. Use a jump ring to attach the heart to a key ring and chain.

Crochet
necklace

This beautiful necklace is a great crochet project for beginners as it uses just one stitch – the chain stitch. For a quick lesson on how to make the stitch, turn to Crochet basics on p.244 before starting work.

To make a crochet necklace you will need

Tools: 2mm (B/1) crochet hook • 1mm (10 steel) crochet hook (if needed) • darning needle
Materials: cotton yarn • approximately 15 beads in different sizes and shapes (ensure the holes are large enough for the beads to pass easily over at least a 1mm (10 steel) crochet hook)

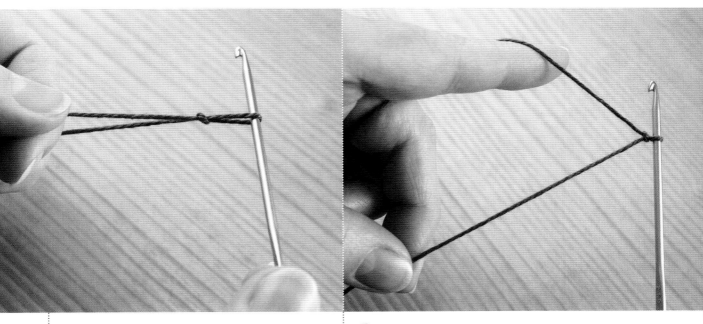

1
Make a slip knot by first crossing the yarn coming from the ball over itself to form a circle. Insert the 2mm (B/1) hook through the circle and pull the ball end through the circle. Tighten.

2
Pull both ends of the yarn firmly to tighten the slip knot around the shank of the hook, ensuring that the knot is tight but not so tight that you can't move it along the hook.

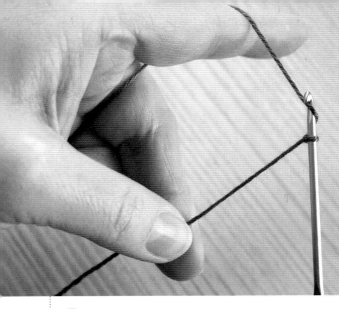

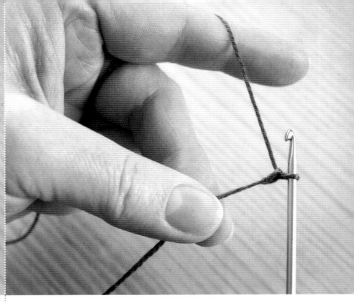

3

To begin the foundation chain, wrap the yarn from the ball around the hook. This action is called "yarn over hook" (abbreviated yo). Use the lip of the hook to grip the yarn as shown.

4

With the lip of the hook, pull the yarn through the loop on the shank of the hook, and tighten it. This makes the first chain of your foundation chain (see p.244).

7

If you switched hooks in Step 6, switch back to the 2mm (B/1) hook. Yo. Grasp the yarn going to the ball with the lip of the hook (see Step 3).

8

Pull the yarn through the loop to secure the bead in place. Continue chaining and adding beads in this way, until the necklace is the length you require.

5

Yo and draw a loop through the loop on the shank of the hook for the next chain. Continue making chains in this way, making a total of 10 to start.

6

Thread a bead onto the hook and insert it back through the loop (see inset). Pass the bead onto the loop, pulling the loop through it. If necessary, use a 1mm (10 steel) hook for this step.

9

Make a slip stitch (ss) (see p.245) in the first chain to join the necklace ends. Cut the yarn, leaving a tail. Pass the tail through the last loop and tighten to finish off.

10

Using a darning needle, work both yarn tails through the chains on either side of the last ss to finish.

Découpage bangle

To make these stylish bangle bracelets, paper cut-outs are glued down and varnished to create a smooth, shiny surface. Almost any paper can be used for this technique, making these bangles the ultimate bespoke gift.

To make a découpage bangle you will need

Tools: ruler • scissors • paintbrushes

Materials: bangle (wooden or plastic) • solid, coloured or patterned backing paper • craft glue • decorative paper motifs • white tack • craft paint • glitter (optional) • clear varnish

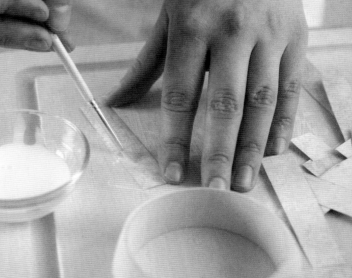

1

Measure the distance around the side of the bangle. Cut paper strips, 1.5cm (⅝in) wide and long enough to wrap around the bangle. Cut enough strips to cover the bangle.

2

Spread glue all over the back of one paper strip, but don't soak it. Position the strip around the edge of the bangle so that the ends overlap on the inside. Remove any air.

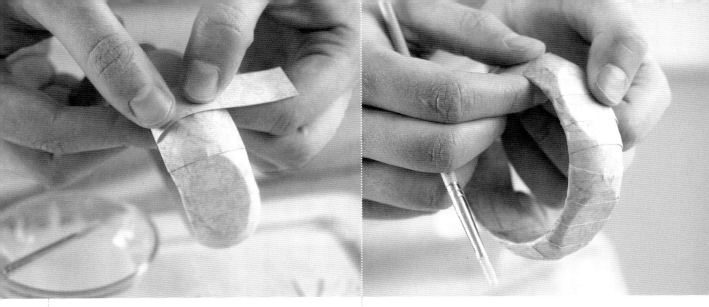

3

Continue adding strips, overlapping slightly with each previous strip, until you have covered the bangle completely with the backing paper.

4

When you have finished this stage, check that each strip of paper is firmly glued down. Smooth out any bumps or wrinkles, adding more glue as necessary.

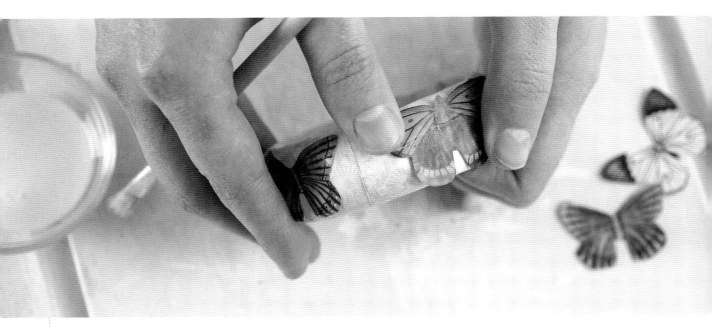

7

Glue the motifs onto the bangle. Take care when sticking down the motifs as they are likely to tear easily when wet with glue, and will be difficult to reposition.

5

Cut another strip of the backing paper for the inside of the bangle. This will need to cover the entire inside surface for a neat finish. Glue in place and leave to dry.

6

Carefully cut out the motifs. Position them around the bangle using white tack, moving them around until you have decided on a design that works for you.

8

Paint a thin border around the top edge of the bangle; leave to dry. Turn the bangle around and paint the other edge. Add glitter, if desired, and leave to dry.

9

Varnish the bangle and leave to dry for two to three days, turning occasionally. When hardened, repeat with a second coat. Leave to dry as before.

Crochet
flower brooches

These pretty crochet flowers would brighten up any jacket or bag. They are more difficult to make than the crochet necklace (pp.70–73), but once you get the hang of it they are quick to create. Make them in different colours, adding a statement button to the centre, for endless variations. You will need to know four different stitches to make these brooches: chain stitch (ch), slip stitch (ss), double crochet (dc), and half treble crochet (htr). For a guide to these stitches, turn to Crochet basics on pp.244–245.

To make a crochet flower brooch you will need

Tools: 4mm crochet hook • sewing needle
Materials: cotton yarn • button • cotton sewing thread • brooch pin

1
Make a slip knot and tighten it (see Steps 1–2 on p.71).

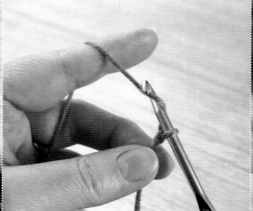

2
To make the first chain (ch) (see p.244) first bring the yarn over the hook (yo).

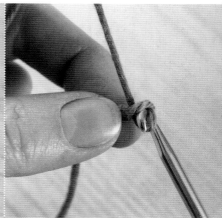

3
Pull the yarn through the loop to make the first ch.

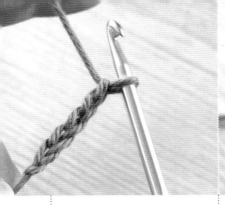

4

Work 5 more ch.

5

Ss (see p.245) into the first chain you made.

6

Tighten the ss to form a circle. Work 1 ch.

10

Work 6 ch.

11

Skip 2 dc and ss into next stitch to create first petal.

14

Work 7 half trebles (htr) (see p.245) into first petal.

15

Work 1 dc into first petal to finish. Then ss into next ch to join.

16

Repeat Steps 13–15 for the other petals. Pull yarn through last loop to finish off.

7

Work 1 dc (see p.244) into the centre of the circle.

8

Continue working 14 more dc into the centre of the circle.

9

Ss into the first dc to join the circle.

12

Repeat Steps 10–11 to create four more petals. Then ss into the first ch to finish round.

13

Work 1 dc into the centre of the first petal.

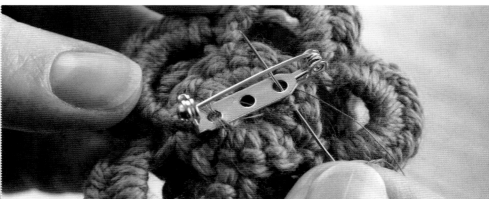

17

Combine two flowers and add a button to the centre.

18

Using sewing cotton, sew a brooch pin to the back of the brooch to complete it.

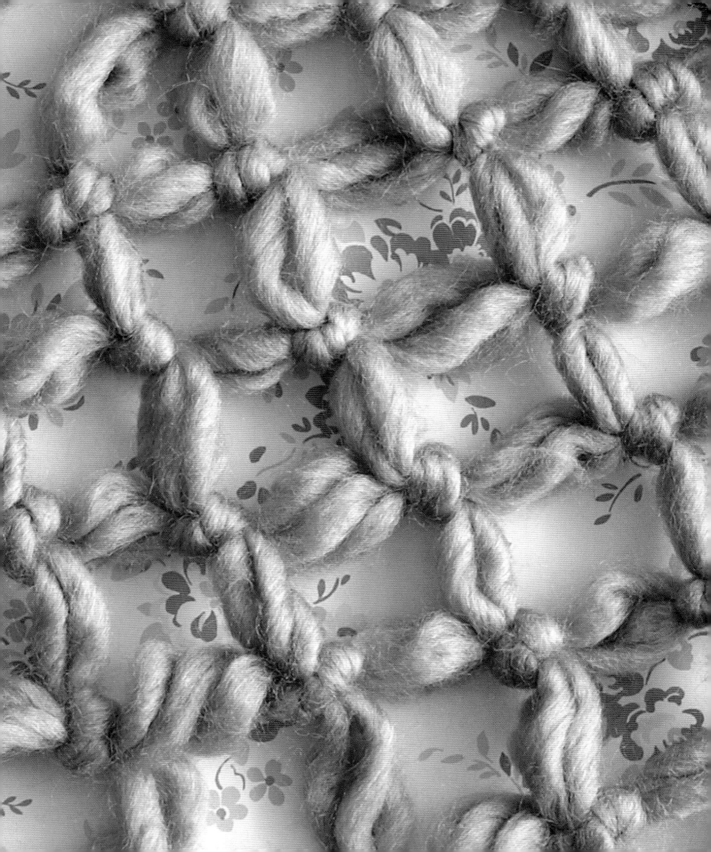

Bags and accessories

All of these bags are made in the same way as the wave-patterned bag on pp.85–87. Turn to pp.88–89 for further instructions, ideas, and inspiration.

Stencilled
bags

Turn plain canvas bags into unique and personal fashion statements with the use of paper stencils and fabric paint. Once you can stencil with confidence, why not try decorating a T-shirt or cushion cover?

To make the wave-patterned bag you will need

Tools: pencil • scalpel • cutting mat • iron • masking tape • plate or palette • sponge • hairdryer • kitchen towel
Materials: tracing paper • stencil paper or card • fabric bag • scrap paper or newspaper • fabric paint in two colours

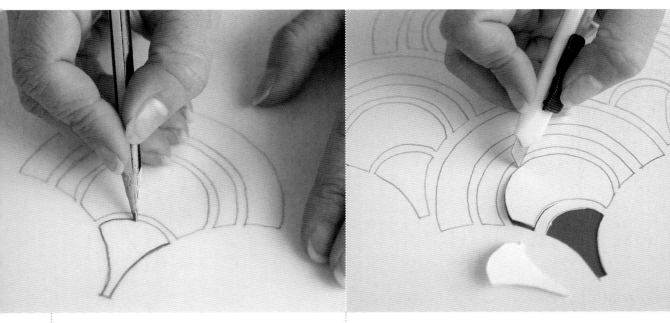

1

Trace the stencil template from p.243 on to tracing paper. Transfer it onto card by flipping the tracing paper over and drawing over the lines while pressing down firmly.

2

Use a scalpel to carefully cut the stencil shape out. If making a repeat pattern, you can cut out the stencil shape a number of times on one sheet, making sure to leave a border of paper.

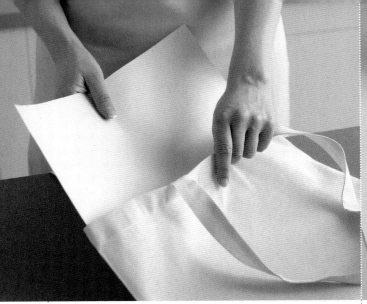

3

Prepare your fabric bag by ironing it, and line the inside with scrap paper or newspaper to stop any excess ink that may soak through the fabric from running through to the back of the bag.

4

Tape down the stencil. Pour some paint on a plate or palette. Dip a clean, dry sponge in the paint, dabbing off any excess. Then apply the paint with the sponge, starting from the centre and working out.

6

Use kitchen towel to blot your stencil and let it dry. You can also prepare more stencils, allowing you to move on with the design while you wait for the first stencil to dry.

7

Once your stencil and fabric paint are dry, reposition your stencil on the bag. Repeat the application process as many times as desired, leaving a few gaps for the second colour.

5

Remove your stencil and put it to one side to dry. Use a hairdryer to dry the paint onto the fabric, ensuring you blow dry the inside of your fabric bag as well as the front so the paint doesn't dry to the lining paper.

8

Once you've stencilled all of the design in one colour and it has dried, apply the second colour in the same way as the first, using a new stencil. Leave to dry overnight.

9

When the fabric paint has fully dried, iron the fabric for a minute or two to fix the paint to the material. You may wish to use a cloth to protect your iron.

Fluttering butterflies

This bag has been stencilled in the same way as the wave-patterned bag on pp.85–87, using the templates on p.243. Butterflies of different shapes and sizes are positioned at slight angles on the same diagonal line, making it look like they are all fluttering in the same direction. Creating the same stencil in different sizes, and overlapping some of the images, also adds a sense of depth to the scene.

The same colour paint has been used to create these butterflies, but you could try stencilling them in a variety of colours for a different look. Alternatively, wait for the design to dry and paint or stencil different coloured markings on the butterflies.

Stitched bag

This large-scale design looks like thread that has been stitched onto the bag, attached to a needle that has also been pushed through the fabric. The look is achieved by creating gaps in the stencil design where the item or object would be obscured by the fabric. Follow the instructions on pp.85–87 to create this look, using the stencils on p.242. Remember to cut separate stencils for different-coloured elements.

Have fun playing with the blank canvas provided by the bag by thinking of other designs that could be interacting with it in some way. For example, you could stencil on a belt going through belt loops, or a ribbon "threaded" through the bag.

Repeated chevrons

This deceptively simple idea results in a striking design with an element of optical illusion. Using the template on p.242, create a stencil, cutting several chevron shapes at equal distances to each other. Following the instructions for the wave-patterned bag on pp.85–87 and starting in the centre of your bag, stencil the pattern onto the bag and dry it. Reposition the stencil so that it continues the chevron pattern as shown, pointing the chevrons the opposite way for every other column, and taking care to keep all the stencilled figures evenly spaced.

Any evenly spaced, repeated pattern makes a striking design, so try this with circles or triangles for a different look. You could also try varying the colours, either according to a pattern or randomly.

Pencil illusion

At first glance it looks like these pencils are complete, but on closer inspection, you can see that only the tip and shaft of the pencil have been stencilled onto the bag. Your eye fills in the rest, completing the image with the background colour. This is a great technique to use for stencilled designs as it can be difficult to stencil very narrow lines or other details needed to complete an image. To make these pencils, use the stencil template on p.242 and follow the instructions for the wave-patterned bag on pp.85–87.

Knotted scarf

Tempted by the balls of soft, luxurious wool in your local haberdashery shop? You can make this cosy scarf without knowing how to knit; simply knot strands of wool together to make this pretty macramé criss-cross design.

To make a knotted scarf you will need

Tools: scissors • 1cm (⅜in)-thick polystyrene foam board (or use a cork pin board) • sewing pins

Materials: 2 x 50g (3½oz) balls Super Chunky wool

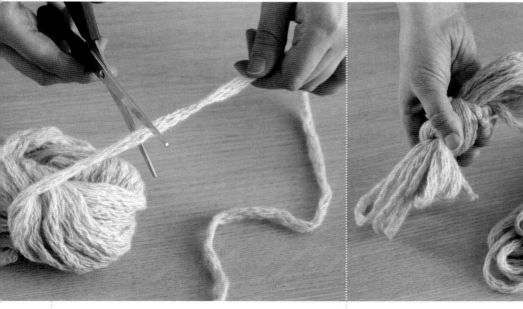

1
Measure and cut the wool into 18 lengths, each about 3.8m (4yd).

2
Arrange the lengths of wool into six groups of three strands each. Wind the wool into bunches and tie loosely, leaving a 50cm (20in) tail; this will make the strands easier to work with.

3

Take the first two bunches and tie them together with a double knot about 12cm (5in) from the top. Repeat with the other bunches, making three knotted sections.

4

Evenly space out the double bunches on a polystyrene foam board or cork pin board. Secure them to the board with a pin through the centre of each knot.

7

Repeat Step 5 to complete the next row of knots. Pin through the new knots to keep the scarf secure and to help space out the knots correctly.

8

Then repeat Step 6. Continue to tie knots in this way until you reach the end of the foam board. Unpin the knots and move the scarf up the board. Repin the last row and continue to knot.

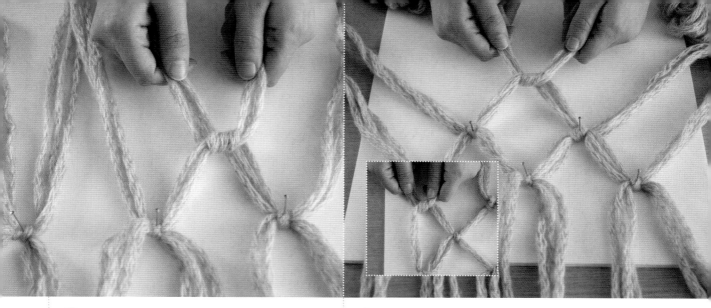

5

Working in bunches of two, knot together the second and third lengths from the left, about 5cm (2in) below the first knot. Repeat with the fourth and fifth lengths. Pin down.

6

Knot together the middle two lengths, again about 5cm (2in) below the previous knot. Then knot each of the sides, keeping the outermost length taut and ensuring the side knots line up with the middle. Pin.

9

When you are about 12cm (5in) from the end of the wool lengths, make a final three knots. Note that you will reach the end of the middle lengths sooner than the sides.

10

Cut all the strands to the same length, and the scarf is complete.

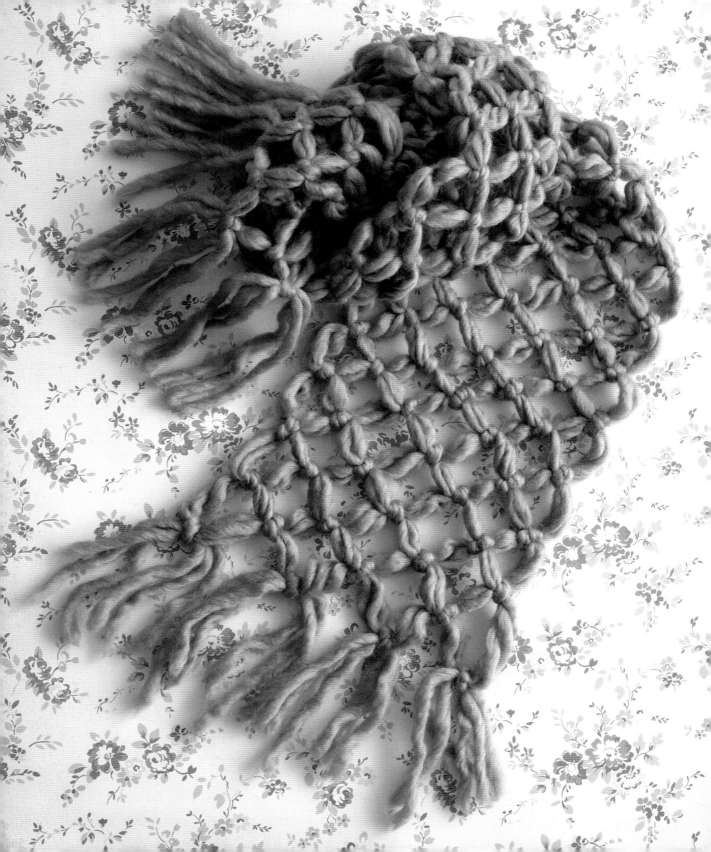

◄ Close-weave scarf

Once you have mastered the technique on pp.91–93, you could reduce the space between the knots and increase the number of bunches for a tighter and thicker finish. This scarf is made with eight bunches of wool, each made up of three strands.

}*Tip: When using two colours, choose the same type of yarn for both so the texture and weight matches.*

Colour-block scarf

Use different colours of wool to add interest to your scarf. Start by pinning the bunches to the board in the order you want them. This scarf is made with eight bunches of wool, each with two strands, and has two bunches of grey either side of four bunches of red.

Clasp-frame
bag

Virtually any fabric can be turned into a stylish, retro-inspired bag or purse by using a clasp frame, available from craft stores and online shops. Different sizes and styles of frames allow you to make bags for different purposes.

To make a clasp-frame clutch bag you will need

Tools: ruler • pencil • dressmaker's scissors • sewing pins • sewing machine or needle

Materials: pattern paper • clasp frame • fabric for outer shell • lining fabric • felt • non-iron interfacing • glue

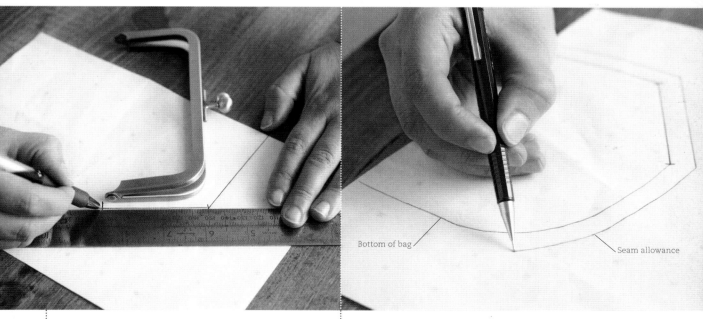

Bottom of bag

Seam allowance

1

Fold the pattern paper in half and draw a line half the length of the frame. From this, draw an angled line the depth of the frame. The angle will depend on how full you want the purse to be.

2

Next draw a line parallel to the first line, where you want the bottom of your bag to be. Join the lines in the shape you want the bag to be and add 1cm ($^1/_2$in) seam allowance.

3

Cut out the template from the folded paper. Unfold it and use it as a guide to cut out two pieces of each of the outer fabric, lining fabric, felt, and interfacing.

4

Create two stacks. In the first, place the outer fabric pieces, right sides facing in between the two felt pieces. In the second, sandwich the lining fabric, right sides facing, between two pieces of interfacing.

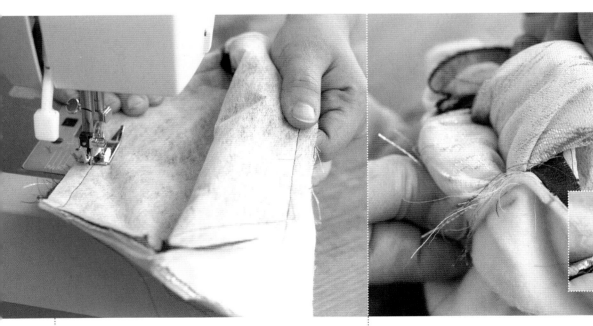

7

Sew around the top of the bag, stopping halfway down one of the long sides to leave a gap so that the purse can be turned right side out. Trim the seams.

8

Turn the purse right side out, and iron it flat. Fold under the edges of the gap, pin it closed, and then topstitch around the top of the purse, closing the gap. This will make it easier to insert into the frame.

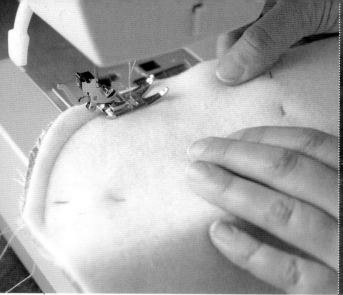

 5

Pin each stack together. Sew around the curved pocket area of each of the stacks. Trim the seams.

 6

Turn the lining piece right side out and place it inside the other piece, making sure it is as deep as it can go, and matching up the side seams.

 9

Put glue on the frame and along the top and sides of the bag. Allow the glue to dry slightly before assembling the bag.

10

Ease the purse into the frame one side at a time, ensuring that the fabric has been pushed right up into the gap. Use a small, flat tool to help if necessary. Leave open to dry for a few hours.

Clasp-frame purse

Perfect for loose change or keeping your MP3 player safe and snug, this snappy little purse has been made using exactly the same technique as the clasp-frame clutch bag on pp.97–99. To create the small, almost-square shape, make sure that all sides of the unfolded template are roughly the same length.

Tip: Use contrasting colours for the outer shell and lining for a fresh, playful look.

Clasp-frame make-up bag

Use a large clasp frame to make the perfect bag for storing make-up or jewellery, in exactly the same way as the clasp-frame clutch bag on pp.97–99. Create a template for a fuller bag by drawing a wider angle for the second line in Step 1, and more room at the bottom by giving the side a steeper curve in Step 2.

Tip: Use fabric from old clothes to make a bag with true vintage appeal.

Painted
silk scarf

It is surprisingly easy to make this beautiful, striped silk scarf. For this method, the silk needs to be suspended in air while it is being painted. If you don't have a silk painting frame, you can suspend it across an old picture frame.

To make a painted silk scarf you will need

Tools: silk painting frame (or medium-sized picture frame) • masking tape • pencil • mixing dishes • square-edged paintbrush

Materials: ready-made silk scarf • tube of water-soluble gutta resist • silk paints in your choice of colours

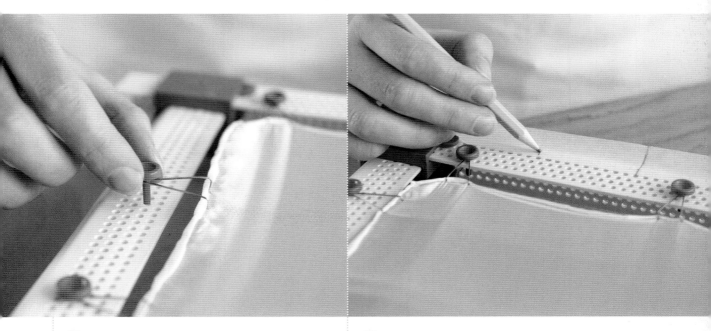

1
Fix the scarf to the silk painting frame. If you are using a picture frame, attach the scarf with masking tape and paint it in sections, moving it along as it dries.

2
Decide how you would like the white stripes on your scarf to be spaced. Stick masking tape down the side of the frame and draw a line for each stripe.

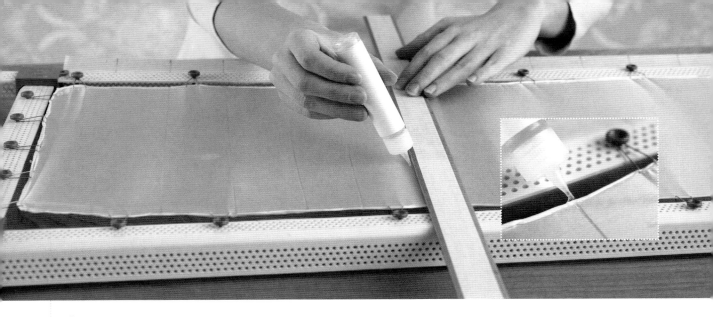

3

With a ruler as a guide, use gutta to draw a line at each marked interval. The gutta will keep the paint colours in each section from running into each other. Ensure that there are no breaks in the lines and that you continue each line all the way to the edge of the fabric (see inset).

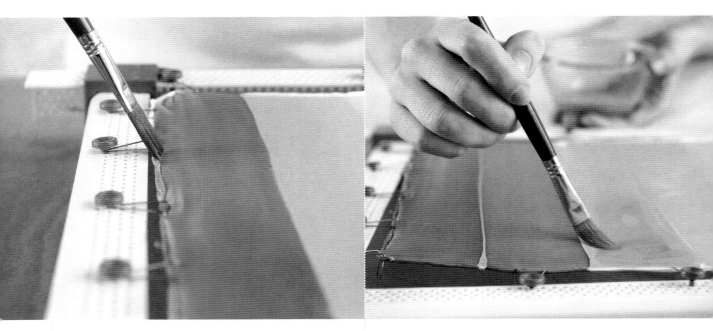

6

Starting with the left-most stripe (right-most if you're left-handed) and using a square-edged brush, paint the first section. Ensure you cover the scarf all the way to the edge.

7

Continue painting stripes in this way, switching colours and working across the scarf. Once finished, leave the scarf to dry.

4

Let the gutta dry and then double-check that there are no breaks in the lines by holding the frame up to the light. Add more gutta to any breaks and allow to dry.

5

Mix your colours. Combine a few drops of each silk colour with 2 tablespoons of water and test the colour on a silk scrap. Adjust the intensity of the colours until you're happy with them.

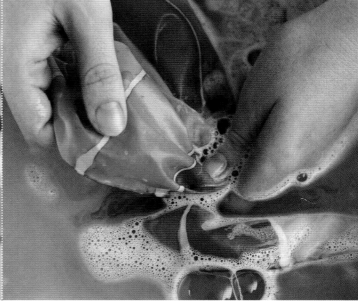

8

Once the scarf has dried completely, remove it from the frame and, following your paint-manufacturer's instructions, iron it on a silk setting to fix the paints.

9

Using a wool and silk detergent, hand-wash the scarf to remove the gutta residue. This will leave behind white lines in the scarf. Leave the scarf to dry, and then iron again.

Make a sleeve for a device of any size by following the instructions for the tablet protector on pp.107–109. Choose the correct-size button to finish it off.

Phone and tablet
protectors

Make a stylish and individual slipcase for a gadget-lover's phone, tablet, or laptop. These instructions are based on the individual device's measurements, and so can be used to make a cover for any make or model.

To make a tablet protector you will need

Tools: tape measure • dressmaker's scissors • iron • ruler • fabric marker • sewing pins • sewing machine or needle
Materials: cotton fabric for the shell • lining fabric • fleece fabric • medium-weight, fusible, woven interfacing • 15cm (5⅞in) round elastic • button • cotton sewing thread

1

Use a tape measure to measure around the length of the device. Divide this number by two, and then add 4.5cm (1¾in). Do the same for the width of the device.

2

Using the measurements from Step 1, draw and cut two rectangles from your chosen shell fabric. Then do the same for the lining fabric, fleece fabric, and fusible woven interfacing.

3

Iron one piece of fusible interfacing to the wrong side of each piece of shell fabric. With the wrong sides facing, lightly iron the lining fabric to the fleece fabric from the side of the lining.

4

Mark a sewing line 1cm (⅜in) from the edge along all four edges of one of the interfaced pieces, on the side of the interfacing. Do the same for one of the fleece and lining pieces, on the fleece side.

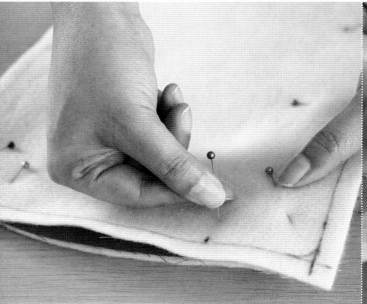

7

Pin the two padded lining pieces together, lining sides facing, marking a 12cm (4¾in) gap along the bottom edge. Sew as in Step 6, leaving a gap. Trim the seams and overstitch the edges.

8

Turn the shell right side out and press. Mark the centre of the top sewing line, mark down 5cm (2in), and sew on the button. Turn wrong side out, add a sewing line to the other side, and mark its centre for the elastic.

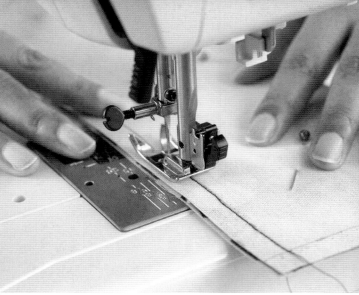

5

Round out the bottom corners of each of the pieces that you have drawn sewing lines on, using a button as a template, and drawing around the button.

6

Pin the two interfaced pieces together, right sides facing and top edges matching. Sew down one side, across the bottom, and up the other side, along the line. Trim the seams and overstitch the edges.

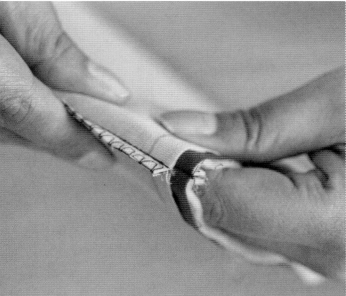

9

Turn the lining right side out. Slide it inside the outer piece. Insert the elastic loop between the two pieces as marked. Pin and sew around the sewing line, double-stitching over the elastic.

10

Trim the seam and overstitch the edges. Reach through the opening in the bottom lining to turn the cover right side out. Stitch closed the gap in the lining by hand. Press the cover.

Pampering gifts

Each of these scented soaps has been made using the method on pp.113–115 and varying the ingredients. See pp.116–119 for variations of the soap recipe.

All natural
luxury soap

Handmade soaps make indulgent gifts, and with the melt-and-pour method require no specialist skill to make. Create naturally scented and coloured soaps using spices, dried fruit or flowers, essential oils, and natural mineral dyes.

To make lemon soap you will need

Tools: gloves • heatproof bowl • pan • spatula • spoon • square mould • knife
Materials: 1kg (2¼lb) white melt-and-pour soap base • ¼–¾ tsp yellow natural mineral colour
• dried lemon peel granules • lemon essential oil • surgical spirit in a spray bottle • 9 dried lemon slices • clingfilm

Makes
9 bars

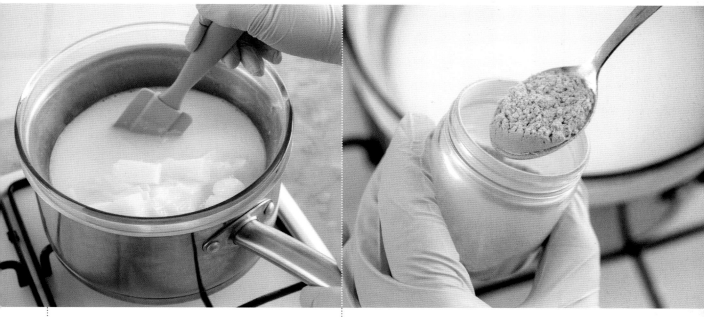

1
Wearing gloves, chop the melt-and-pour soap into pieces and heat in a heatproof bowl over a pan of boiling water, stirring occasionally, until all lumps have melted.

2
Add the desired amount of colouring to the melted soap base and stir until the powder has mixed in and the colour is evenly distributed.

113

3

Add the lemon peel granules a little at a time, stirring gently. Continue stirring until the granules are spread evenly throughout the soap mixture.

4

Just before you pour the soap mixture into the mould, slowly add the essential oil and stir gently until it is evenly distributed throughout.

7

Spray the almost-set layer again with surgical spirit. This will act as a glue and help it to bond to the next layer of soap.

8

Slowly pour the remaining mixture into the mould and add the dried lemon slices. You will need to act fast, as the top layer will begin to set as soon as it is poured in.

5

Pour approximately three-quarters of the mixture into the mould. Leave the remainder in the bowl over the hot water to keep it melted and warm.

6

Spray the mixture with surgical spirit to remove any bubbles. Leave this first layer for 20–25 minutes until it is almost set. It should be hard but warm.

9

Create a 3 x 3 pattern so that each slice of soap will contain a lemon slice. Spritz the surface with surgical spirit to remove any bubbles and leave until hard.

10

Remove the soap from the mould and cut it with a knife into nine even squares. Wrap each square in clingfilm to prevent it attracting moisture.

Pampering
gifts

Soap recipe variations

∙∙∙

Make a variety of soaps by choosing different scent
and colour combinations. All these soaps are made
in the same way as the lemon soap (see pp.113–115),
using 1kg (2¼lb) of white melt-and-pour soap base
and make nine square bars of soap.

A. *Bergamot soap*
¼–¾ tsp orange natural mineral colour
2½ tsp bergamot essential oil
9 whole dried orange slices

B. *Rose soap*
2½ tsp rose absolute diluted in 5% grapeseed oil
100g (3½oz) rose buds

C. *Cinnamon soap*
¼–¾ tsp caramel natural mineral colour
2½ tsp cinnamon leaf essential oil
9 cinnamon sticks

D. *Camomile soap*
¼–¾ tsp dark green natural mineral colour
2½ tsp camomile essential oil
35g (1¼oz) dried camomile flowers

E. *Lavender soap*
¼–¾ tsp purple natural mineral colour
2½ tsp English lavender essential oil
10g (¼oz) dried lavender

F. *Vanilla soap*
¼–¾ tsp cream natural mineral colour
2½ tsp vanilla essential oil
30g (1oz) vanilla pods (use the seeds in the mixture)

G. *Juniper soap*
¼–¾ tsp pink natural mineral colour
2½ tsp juniper essential oil
100g (3½oz) juniper berries

H. *Sandalwood soap*
¼–¾ tsp light brown natural mineral colour
2½ tsp sandalwood fragrance
50g (1¾oz) blue poppy seeds

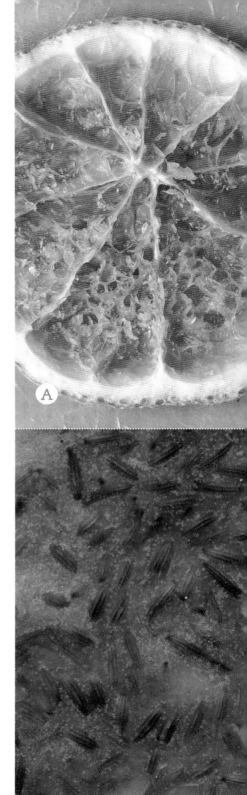

A

E

Juniper cake-slice soap

You will need

1kg (2¹/₄lb) white melt-and-pour soap base
¹/₄ tsp pink natural mineral colour
2¹/₂ tsp juniper essential oil
100g (3¹/₂oz) juniper berries

This soap cake is made like the lemon soap on pp.113–115, but in two stages. First, melt half the soap, adding the pink colour and half the essential oil. Pour it into a round container and let it set, spritzing it with surgical spirit to get rid of any bubbles. Melt the second half of the soap, adding the remaining scent. Spritz the base again, and pour on the second layer of soap. Add the juniper berries to the top, spritzing it one final time to get rid of any remaining bubbles. Once set, remove from the mould and cut into slices.

Moulded vanilla stars

You will need

1kg (2¹/₄lb) white melt-and-pour soap base
¹/₄–³/₄ tsp cream natural mineral colour
2¹/₂ tsp vanilla essential oil
30g (1oz) vanilla pods

These vanilla-scented stars are made in the same way as the lemon soap on pp.113–115, but the mixture is poured into individual moulds to set. Soap moulds are sold in craft shops, or you could use silicone cake moulds. Vanilla seeds are used instead of lemon peel granules as an exfoliant and for added scent. Vanilla pods can also be used to decorate the tops of the stars by placing them into the mould before the mixture is poured on top.

Cookie-cutter lavender hearts

You will need
1kg (2¼lb) white melt-and-pour soap base
¼–¾ tsp purple natural mineral colour
2½ tsp lavender essential oil
10g (¼oz) dried lavender

These heart-shaped soaps are made
using the same method and quantity
of ingredients as the Lemon soap on
pp.113–115, swapping in the ingredients
above. However, instead of cutting the
soap into squares, they are cut with
heart-shaped cookie cutters. The
lavender buds will float to the top,
creating an exfoliating layer.

See-through orange soap

You will need
1kg (2¼lb) clear melt-and-pour soap base
2½ tsp bergamot essential oil
9 dried orange slices

Although made in the same way as the
lemon soap on pp.113–115, using a clear
soap base and adding a dried orange slice
inside the soap gives these soaps a fresh
look. Make them by first melting half of
the clear soap base, and adding half of the
essential oil. Pour the mixture into a square
mould, and add the orange slices evenly to
the top. Allow this layer to set before melting
the remaining half of the soap base and
adding the remaining essential oil. Spritz
the set layer with surgical spirit and add
the melted soap mixture to the top. Spritz
again to get rid of any bubbles and allow
to set. Cut the soap into nine square bars.

Manicure
roll

Use gorgeous Thai silk or pretty cotton for this manicure roll. Fill the pockets with nailcare essentials and add a couple of beautiful polishes to complete the gift. The recipient should feel very pampered!

To make a manicure roll you will need

Tools: dressmaker's scissors • steam iron • sewing machine • sewing pins
Materials: patterned silk-mix fabric • plain silk-mix lining fabric • iron-on interfacing
• ribbon • cotton tape • matching cotton sewing threads

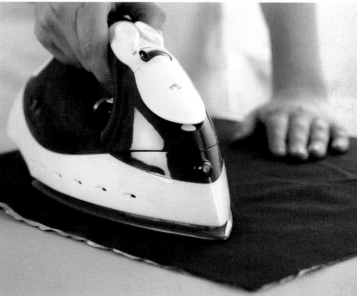

1

Cut one 38 x 43cm (15 x 17in) piece each from the main patterned fabric, the lining fabric, and the iron-on interfacing.

2

Lay the main fabric right-side down and place the interfacing on top. Iron to secure. Machine sew using zigzag or overlock stitch around the edge.

3

Using the zigzag setting, machine sew around the lining fabric to prevent fraying. Place the main and lining fabric together, right sides facing, and sew along the two long edges and one short edge.

4

Turn the fabric right side out. Fold the sides of the open seam inwards. Press and pin. Topstitch along the edge to close.

7

Starting from one of the bottom corners of the pocket, topstitch along the edge, securing the side of the pocket and the ribbon in place. Continue stitching up around the top of the flap, and down the other side, securing the other side of the pocket.

5

Fold the topstitched edge over 11cm (4½in) from the bottom. Cut 41cm (16in) of ribbon and pin it across the pocket, folding and pinning the edges under the pocket.

6

Fold the rest of the ribbon in half and pin the end into the top left corner of the pocket, under the folded edge.

8

Choose how wide you would like the pocket divisions to be and mark them using cotton tape. Pin the tape into position.

9

Machine sew the pockets, using the cotton tape as a guideline. Remove the pins and tape and the manicure roll is ready to fold and tie up with the ribbon tie.

Container candles

A homemade candle can be made into an extra special gift by putting it in a pretty teacup or a handy travel-size tin. Add colour and fragrance to complement the container or the recipient.

To make a teacup candle you will need

Tools: double boiler (or large saucepan and heatproof bowl) • craft thermometer • heat-resistant mat or rack • metal spoon • 2 wooden skewers • 2 elastic bands *Materials:* teacup • soy wax flakes (the weight of wax in grams = the volume of water the container holds in ml) • wax dye • wick • wick sustainer

1
Boil water in the lower pan of a double boiler and add wax flakes to the top pan. Alternatively, use a heatproof bowl over a saucepan. Heat the wax, stirring occasionally.

2
When the wax has melted and reached a temperature of 70°C (158°F), take the pan off the heat and add the dye – 1g (¹⁄₁₆oz) for each 100g (3½oz) of wax. Stir until dissolved.

3

While the wax is heating, prepare the wick. Attach the wick sustainer (a metal tab) to a length of wick and place in the teacup. Secure the ends of the two skewers with elastic bands and insert the wick between them. Rest the skewers on the rim of the cup and pull the wick gently to ensure it is taut and centred in the cup.

4

Slowly pour the melted wax into the cup and tap it with a spoon to release air bubbles. Allow the candle to cool, add more wax if it has shrunk, then trim the wick when the candle has set.

Scented candles

There are two types of fragrance oil: candle fragrance oil (a synthetic blend) and essential/aromatherapy oil (extracted from plants and flowers, and 100% natural). Both types are stirred into the hot wax just before pouring. Try these different aromatherapy scents to enhance your mood:

A. *Pine or clove*
To increase energy

B. *Lavender or neroli*
To calm, soothe, and relax

C. *Jasmine or bergamot*
To uplift the mood and spirit

D. *Cinnamon or eucalyptus*
To promote concentration

E. *Sandalwood or lemon*
To relieve stress

Travel candles

Handy travel candles can be made in small tins or glass jars with lids.
Create them in the same way as the teacup candle (see pp.125–126).
If you are using different colours or scents, you will need to divide the
hot wax into batches before stirring in the dye or fragrance oil for each
tin. After the candle has set, decorate or label the container as desired.
These candles have each been decorated with beads threaded on a wire
and a label made out of thick foil and embossed from the other side.

Layered candles

To make these layered candles, follow the instructions for making the teacup candle (see pp.125–126). Divide the melted wax into batches – one for each colour you want – and stir in the dyes. With the wick in place, pour the first layer of coloured wax into the glass, tap to release air bubbles, and allow to set. When it is solid to the touch, reheat the next batch of wax and pour in, and repeat for each layer. Leave for 24 hours until fully set.

Tip: Produce darker shades of the same colour by increasing the quantity of dye used in each batch.

Candles in ramekins

Ramekins – small dishes that are usually used for individual pudding portions – are ideal for making a set of candles to give as a gift. The ramekins can be washed and reused as long as the candles have been made with soy wax flakes. (Alternatively, pop them in a freezer for a few hours and the wax should drop out.) Use the method for making the teacup candle on pp.125–126.

Three-wick candle

This impressive three-wick candle can be
created in the same way as the teacup candle
(see pp.125–126), but you will need another
set of skewers to hold the third wick (you
should be able to get two wicks into the
first set). Multi-wick candles give off more
fragrance as well as more light.

*Tip: Ceramic bowls
or long, narrow plant
containers can also be used
for multi-wick candles.*

Oilcloth
wash bag

Fill this wash bag with shredded tissue and cosmetics for the perfect pampering gift. The bag is made from oilcloth to make it water resistant, but you could use a sturdy cotton fabric or even quilted cotton for a different look.

To make an oilcloth wash bag you will need

Tools: rotary cutter and mat (or dressmaker's scissors) • sewing pins • sewing machine or needle

Materials: oilcloth • cotton lining fabric • 30cm (12in) zip • cotton sewing thread to match the lining fabric

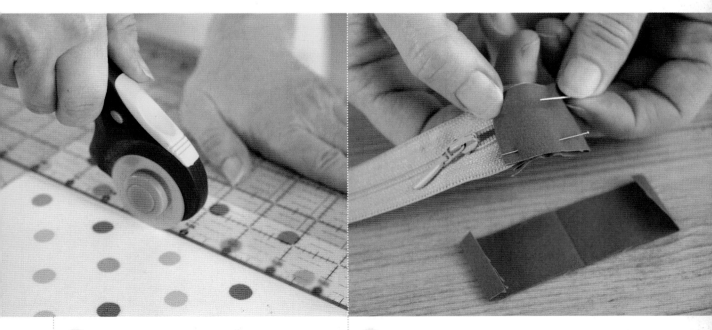

1

Cut two pieces of your chosen outer fabric and two pieces of lining, each 20 x 30cm (8 x 12in). Cut two more pieces of lining fabric, each 9 x 2.5cm (3½ x 1in).

2

Fold over 5mm (¼in) of each end of the small lining strips. Fold one piece over the end of the zip, pin in place, and stitch across all layers. Repeat for the other end.

131

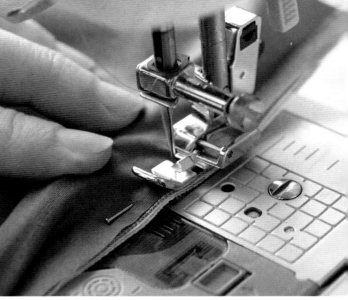

3

Layer one piece of oilcloth, facing up, with the zip, facing down, and the lining, facing down. Pin. Then pin the other edge of the zip to the other oilcloth and lining pieces in the same way.

4

Stitch through all three layers along each side of the zip, using a long stitch and the correct zip foot for your machine. Make sure that you hold the layers not being stitched out of the way of the needle.

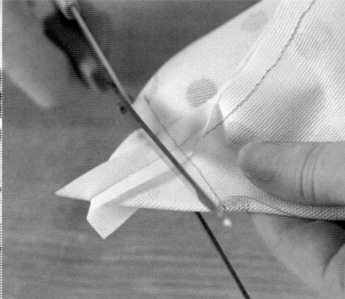

7

Ensure the zip is three-quarters open. Stitch around the edge of the lining and oilcloth, leaving a gap in the lining. When you come to the seams, flatten them to reduce bulk.

8

Shape all four corners by re-folding each corner so that the seam is now in the middle of the new corner. Fold open the seam and stitch across, 3cm (1¼in) up from the corner. Trim off the corner.

5

Use your finger to smooth along the line of the zip, pushing the fabric out. If needed, you can iron the seams on a very low setting, from the lining side protecting it with a tea towel.

6

Next, bring the right sides of the oilcloth and lining pieces together. Pin the two lining pieces together, leaving a 10cm (4in) gap at the bottom edge. You don't need to pin the oilcloth.

9

Reach through the gap in the lining to turn out the bag, pushing out the corners. If needed, iron on a very low setting from the inside, using a tea towel to protect the bag.

10

Finally, fold under the edges of the gap in the lining, and iron them so that they meet neatly. Then pin and stitch the lining closed either by hand or machine.

Follow instructions on pp.135–137 to make the juniper bath bomb. Make a rose bath bomb the same way, but using rose essential oil and adding rose petals.

Fizzy bath bombs

Bath bombs are solid balls that fizz and bubble as they dissolve, adding scent and colour to the bath water. They make wonderful gifts and are surprisingly easy to make with ingredients that are readily available at most supermarkets.

To make a juniper bath bomb you will need

Tools: sieve • 1 medium mixing bowl • 2 small mixing bowls • spoon • bath bomb mould
Materials: 155g (5½oz) bicarbonate of soda • 75g (2½oz) citric acid • ¼ tsp purple natural mineral colour • ½ tsp juniper essential oil • water in a spray bottle

Makes 1 bath bomb

1

Measure out the bicarbonate of soda and sieve it into the larger mixing bowl.

2

Add the citric acid to the bicarbonate of soda and mix well with your fingers until fully combined.

3

Split the mixture between the two smaller bowls. Add the colour to the first bowl and mix well with a spoon or your fingers, ensuring no lumps remain.

4

Add approximately half the fragrance to the first bowl and half to the second bowl. Mix each bowl well, again making sure that no lumps remain.

7

Add white mixture to the mould half, leaving a mound at the top. Repeat the process for the other mould half, this time starting with the white mixture.

8

Bring the two mould halves together, making sure that the two halves of the bath bomb are lined up exactly. Press the halves together.

 5

Spray both bowls lightly with water and mix it in evenly with your fingers. Continue to spritz and mix until the mixture feels damp but not too moist.

 6

Fill one of the mould halves halfway with the purple mixture. Gently press the mixture down into the mould with your fingers to remove any pockets of air.

 9

Leave the bath bomb to set for approximately five minutes. Try not to move it at all during this time, as it can be very fragile before it is set.

 10

Once set, first remove one of the mould halves. Then place your palm over the bath bomb and gently turn it over. Remove the other mould half.

Sweet dreams
eye mask

Sweet dreams are guaranteed with this eye mask, made using blackout fabric to ensure no light passes through. You could also put a little dried lavender inside before you sew up the mask, to add a lovely scent when the mask is used.

To make an eye mask you will need

Tools: dressmaker's scissors • sewing pins • sewing machine • sewing needle • safety pin

Materials: patterned cotton fabric • cotton lining fabric • blackout fabric • cotton sewing thread to match the binding and the main fabric • 50cm (20in) of 15mm (½in) bias binding in a matching colour • 40cm (16in) of 12mm (½in) elastic

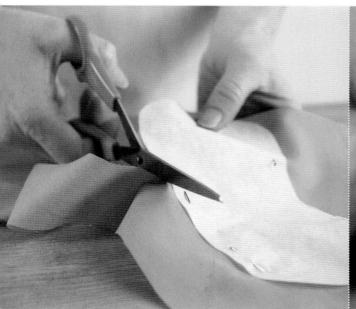

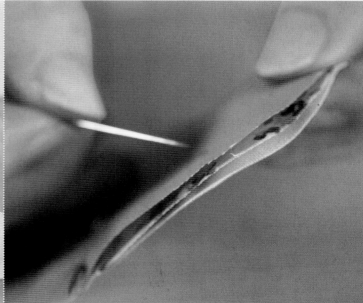

1
Photocopy or trace the eye mask template (see p.232). Cut one eye mask shape from the main fabric, one from the lining, and one from the blackout fabric.

2
Place the main fabric, right side up, on top of the blackout fabric. Place the lining fabric, right side down, on top of the main fabric. Pin all three layers together.

3

Stitch around the edge, beginning and ending so that you leave a 5cm (2in) gap along the straight top edge. Reverse stitch at the beginning and end to secure the stitching.

4

Trim the seam allowance all around the mask to remove the excess fabric and neaten the edge. Then turn the mask right side out. Iron it flat.

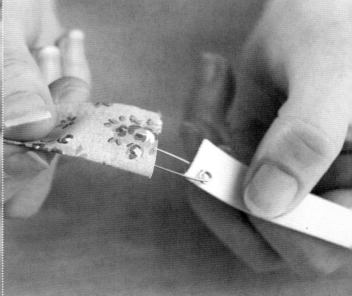

7

Cut out a 6.5 x 50cm (2½ x 20in) piece of fabric for the casing. Fold the piece in half lengthways, and fold the edges under again. Iron flat. Pin and stitch the long edge closed.

8

Attach a safety pin to one end of the elastic and a large straight pin to the other to stop the end slipping into the casing. Use the safety pin to help push the elastic through.

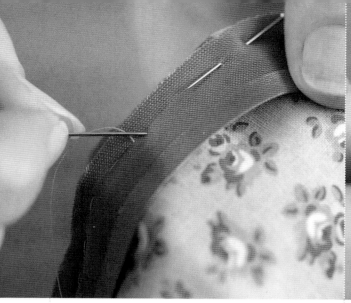

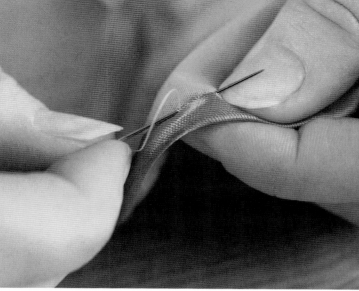

5

Open the bias binding and pin it onto the front of the mask, right side to right side, placing the pins on the fold line closest to the edge. Stitch along the fold line using a running stitch.

6

When you reach the end of the bias, fold the short edge under and stitch it over where you began for a neat finish. Then fold the binding over to the back of the mask and slip stitch in place.

9

Once the elastic is all the way through, stitch both ends of the elastic to the casing. Fold over the end of the strap to hide the raw edge, and handstitch to the back of the mask.

10

Flip the mask over, and stitch along the edge where the elastic meets the bias edging. Repeat Steps 9–10 for the other end of the strap to finish the mask.

Pamper hamper

Surprise a friend in need of pampering with a hamper full of handmade, all-natural goodies. Any of the items in the Pampering section would make great hamper fillers. Our basket contains a set of all-natural luxury soaps (pp.112–117) packaged together in a box, a slice of juniper soap (p.118), a striped juniper bath bomb and a rose petal one (pp.134–137), an oilcloth washbag (pp.130–133), and a sweet dreams eye mask (pp.138–141). Round out the hamper with other inexpensive pampering items such as brushes, sponges, loofahs, and towels. You could even add bath salts in a glass jar. Wrap the hamper in cellophane and tie it off with a ribbon or two for a truly luxurious handmade gift.

For pet lovers

Cat's playmat

For the cat who has everything! This mat will keep your feline friend busy and would also make a luxurious lining for a cat basket, or could be thrown over a favourite chair or sofa. For added appeal, fill the toys with catnip.

To make a cat playmat you will need

Tools: scissors • sewing pins • sewing machine • sewing needle • embroidery hoop *Materials:* metallic fabric in orange and silver • thin cord • stuffing • cotton sewing threads • white and black buttons • small bells • feathers • white embroidery thread • wadding • patterned cotton fabric • gingham fabric • orange bias binding • metal rings

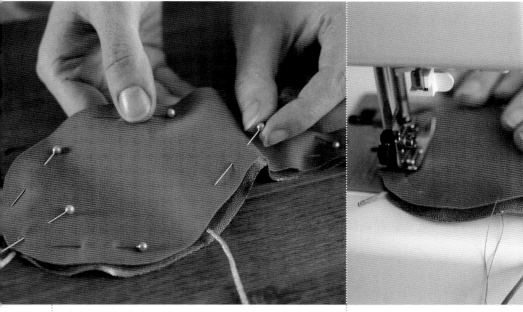

1
Using the template on p.233, cut two sides for each fish from two pieces of orange fabric held right sides together. Pin. Pin the end of 20cm (8in) thin cord to the mouth as shown.

2
Machine sew around the edges, 5mm (¼in) from the edge, securing the cord at the mouth. Leave a 2cm (¾in) gap, allowing the rest of the cord to pass through the gap.

 3

Turn the fish right side out. You should have the long length of cord (the "fishing line") hanging from the mouth. Stitch several times through the cord to make it secure.

4

Push stuffing into the fish and sew the opening shut using neat overstitching and matching thread. Repeat to make another fish. Make a fish hook in the same way, using the silver metallic fabric.

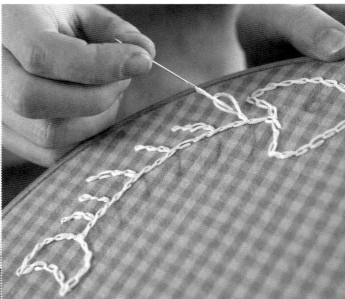

 7

Cut a square of gingham fabric and a square of patterned fabric, each 70 x 70cm (27½ x 27½ in). Cut the wadding so it is about 3mm (⅛in) smaller all the way around than the fabric squares.

8

Place the gingham fabric in the embroidery hoop and tighten. Use the template on p.233 to draw a pencil outline of a fish skeleton and use chain stitch and white embroidery thread to go over the design.

 5

Sew a white and black button either side of each fish head. Make sure they are attached securely. Alternatively, embroider eyes using embroidery thread.

6

Thread and knot a bell to the fishing line about 5cm (2in) from the fish's mouth. Using embroidery thread, tightly bind a feather to the fishing line, just above the bell.

9

Layer the fabrics – gingham, wadding, then patterned cotton – and pin together. Pin the bias binding around the edge and machine sew through it to sew the layers together.

10

Attach metal rings to two of the edges and one corner of the mat using cotton thread. Tie the fishes and hook securely to the rings.

Catnip mice

For pet lovers

Filled with catnip, these little mice make a delightful gift that a cat literally cannot resist. This is a great project for using up offcuts and leftover pieces of material. Cotton fabrics work well, but why not also try tweed or leather?

To make a catnip mouse you will need

Tools: dressmaker's scissors • pencil • sewing pins • sewing machine • sewing needle
Materials: cotton fabric • felt fabric in two different colours • white wool yarn • wadding
• cotton sewing thread • dried catnip (optional) • black embroidery thread

1
Using the template on p.231, cut out two main body pieces from two pieces of fabric held right sides together. Cut out the base and ears from coloured felt.

2
Cut three lengths of wool to twice as long as you would like the tail to be and knot them together. Knot the short ends around a pencil and make a plait to use for the tail.

151

3

Pin the body pieces together, right side to right side. Start sewing 8mm (⅜in) in from the bottom edge. Sew around the curve, stopping 8mm (⅜in) from the end.

4

Tie off the ends and trim the excess fabric to make the seam less bulky once the mouse is turned right side out.

7

Trim off the excess fabric in the seams and turn the mouse right side out, pushing the nose out with your finger. If necessary, use a needle to pull out the tip from the outside.

8

Push small amounts of wadding into the mouse, ensuring that you fill the nose. When it is half stuffed, add dried catnip. Finish stuffing the mouse.

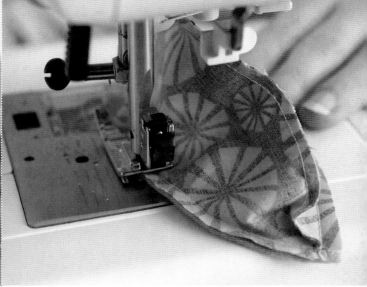

5

Pin the felt base to the long sides of the body pieces, so that the right side of each of the pieces is facing the felt base.

6

Starting from the back end (the slightly raised end) of the mouse, stitch all the way around the sides, attaching the top layer to the base, and stopping 2.5cm (1in) before the end.

9

Insert the tail underneath the back seam, pinning the seam closed. Using small stitches, carefully sew up the opening, securing the tail into position.

10

Bring one cut edge of the ear over the other so that the ear curves inward. Pin in place and stitch down, repeating for the other side. Embroider two black eyes onto the mouse.

Dog biscuits

These homemade dog biscuits are sure to go down a treat! What's more, they are made from all natural ingredients so they are good for your dog, and they contain parsley to help freshen his breath, too.

To make dog biscuits you will need

Tools: baking tray • greaseproof paper • 2 mixing bowls • tablespoon • chopping knife • grater • wooden spoon • rolling pin • bone-shaped cookie cutter (or knife) • cooling rack *Ingredients:* chicken stock (cube or granules) • a large handful of parsley • 1 medium-sized carrot • 75g (2½oz) cheese • 1 tbsp olive oil • 240g (8oz) wholewheat flour • 75g (2½oz) oats • 1 tsp baking powder

1
Heat the oven to 180°C (350°F). Grease a baking tray and line it with greaseproof paper.

2
Make up double-strength chicken stock and leave it to cool. You could also use homemade stock.

3

Chop the parsley. Grate the carrot and cheese. You could use pre-grated cheese for this step if you prefer.

4

Mix the parsley, carrot, and cheese together in a bowl. Add the oil and combine well, until all the ingredients are coated.

7

Sprinkle some flour on the work surface and shape the dough into a flat disc with your hands. Using a rolling pin, roll out the dough to the desired thickness.

8

Use a cookie cutter (or knife) to cut shapes from the dough. Combine the offcuts, roll again, and cut out more shapes until no dough remains.

5

In a separate bowl, combine the flour, oats, and baking powder. Mix them together well.

6

Combine the parsley, carrot, and cheese mixture with the flour mixture. Add the stock one tablespoon at a time to make the mixture moist. Knead with your hands to make a dough.

9

Bake for 25–30 minutes, until golden brown. Move to a wire rack and cool completely.

Simple silhouette

An even easier way to create an appliqué keepsake of your pet is to cut out a side-on silhouette from one fabric. Do this by enlarging a profile photograph on a photocopier to use as a template. You can make this floral pup using the template on p.231.

Appliqué pet portrait

Use the appliqué technique to create a stunning portrait of a beloved pet, perfect for decorating a cushion or displaying in a frame. Use the cat template provided, or make your own from a favourite photograph.

To make an appliqué pet portrait cushion cover you will need

Tools: iron • dressmaker's scissors • sewing needle • sewing pins • sewing machine

Materials: bonding web • black, grey, and white fabric • cushion cover • contrast cotton sewing thread for tacking • blue, pink, and black felt • black and white cotton sewing thread

1
Re-size the template (see p.230) to fit your cushion cover. Transfer the head piece on to bonding web, and iron it on to the reverse of your selected fabric.

2
Repeat the process for the back, chest, ear, and muzzle pieces. Then cut out each element. Note that the eyes and nose don't need to be faced.

159

3

Carefully peel off the backing paper from all the faced pieces.

4

Assemble the pieces on the cushion cover. Make sure the head piece overlaps the chest piece and the back piece. Iron in place.

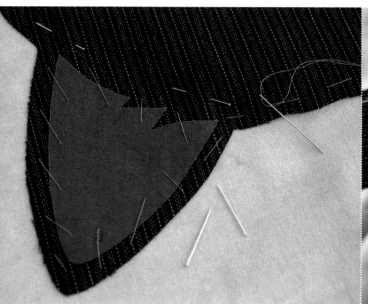

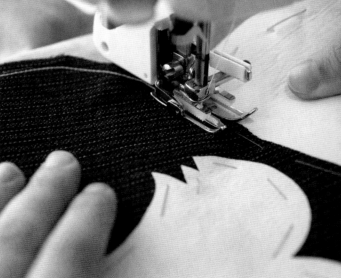

7

Pin, then tack the pieces, except the eyes and nose, in place on the cushion cover. Remove the pins.

8

Sew around the outside of each of the tacked pieces about 5mm (¼in) from the edge, either by hand or with a sewing machine. Remove the tacking thread.

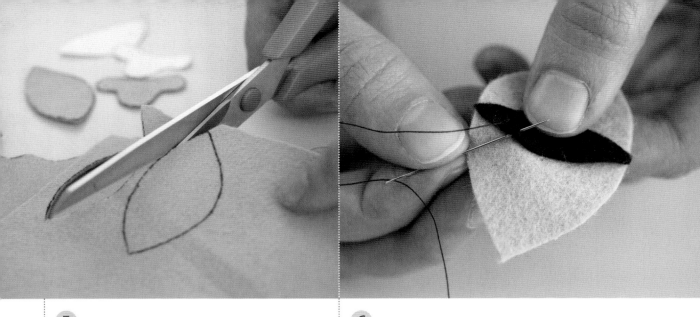

 5
Trace the eyes, nose, and pupils on to coloured felt and cut them out.

 6
Stitch pupils on to the eye pieces using tiny backstitches and black thread.

 9
Tack the eyes and nose on to the cat's face and stitch around the edges of each piece. Remove the tacking thread.

 10
Using the image on p.158 as a guide, sew guidelines for the whiskers and eyelashes using tacking thread. Stitch over them using topstitch. Remove the tacking threads.

Tartan
dog jacket

Keep a favourite dog warm and cosy all winter long with this easy-to-make, fleece-lined jacket. You can adjust the pattern to make it in any size. It fastens with Velcro, making it easy to put on and take off.

To make a tartan dog jacket you will need

Tools: tracing paper • dressmaker's scissors • sewing pins • sewing machine

Materials: tartan check fabric • wadding • interfacing • fleece fabric • cotton sewing threads • Velcro • red grosgrain ribbon

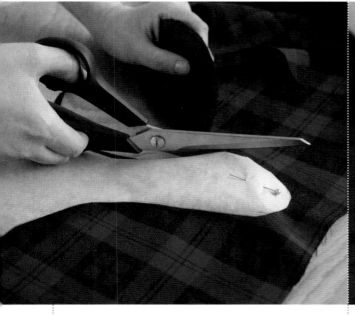

1

Using the template on pp.234–235, use tracing paper to make a pattern and adjust it to fit your dog. Cut out one jacket piece and one belly strap from each fabric.

2

Place the check fabric, right side out, on top of the wadding and interfacing. Pin all three layers together.

3

Machine sew along the lines of the check fabric using a long stitch, first in one direction and then the other. This quilts the jacket.

6

Machine sew around the edges of the jacket, joining the upper and lining pieces. Neaten the edges with a zigzag or overlock stitch.

7

Pin the grosgrain ribbon around the jacket as shown. Machine sew around the ribbon to attach. Fold the other half of the ribbon over the edge, and topstitch or hand stitch to attach.

 4

Pin Velcro onto the lining and
the quilted upper at the points
marked on the template. Stitch
the Velcro into place.

 5

Pin the quilted upper and
the fleece lining together,
right sides out.

 8

Make the belly strap in the same way as
the jacket, attaching Velcro to the belly
strap as indicated on the template. Pin the
two sections as shown and stitch together.

Edible gifts

Butter biscuits

Deliciously light and crumbly butter biscuits make a lovely gift on their own, but they are also a very versatile biscuit base. Why not try icing them or adding chocolate and chopped nuts (see p.172) for a gourmet twist?

To make plain butter biscuits you will need

Tools: large mixing bowl • wooden spoon • rolling pin • palette knife • clingfilm • round pastry cutter • non-stick baking sheets • wire cooling rack *Ingredients:* 100g (3½oz) caster sugar • 225g (8oz) plain flour, sifted, plus extra for dusting • 155g (5½oz) unsalted butter, softened and diced • 1 egg yolk • 1 tsp vanilla extract

Makes 30 biscuits

1

Preheat the oven to 180°C (350°F/Gas 4). Put the sugar, flour, and butter into a large mixing bowl, or into the bowl of a food processor.

2

Rub together, or pulse blend, the ingredients until they look like fine breadcrumbs.

169

3

Add the egg yolk and vanilla extract, and combine together until the mixture forms a dough.

6

Flour the dough and the work surface well, and roll the dough out to a thickness of about 5mm (¼in). Use a palette knife to move the dough to prevent it sticking.

7

If the dough is too sticky to roll well, wrap it in clingfilm and chill for 15 minutes, then try again.

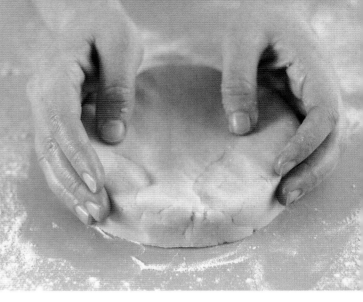

4

Turn the dough out onto a floured surface and knead it briefly until smooth.

5

Shape the dough into a round, flat disc with your hands.

8

With the pastry cutter, cut out round biscuits.

9

Transfer the biscuits to the baking sheets with a palette knife. Re-roll the pastry offcuts to 5mm (¼in) thick. Cut out biscuits until all the dough is used up.

10

Bake in batches for 10–15 minutes until golden brown at the edges. Remove from the oven and leave the biscuits to cool on the baking sheet until firm enough to handle.

11

Once firm enough, transfer the biscuits to a wire rack. Allow to cool completely before serving. The biscuits will keep well in an airtight container for five days.

Butter biscuit variations

Add chocolate, raisins, and chopped nuts to the basic recipe to create butter biscuits with a "wow" factor. Divide the dough into three parts after Step 3 and add the ingredients listed below to each batch. Add the raisins and chocolate directly to each batch of dough, roll, and cut out. Sprinkle the nuts and more chocolate chunks on top. Bake as directed and allow to cool. Pack them in a tin or box up with tissue paper for a gourmet gift.

A. 1 tbsp chopped pistachio nuts and 1 tbsp white chocolate chunks

B. 2 tbsp raisins and 2 tbsp chopped hazelnuts

C. 3 tbsp dark chocolate chunks

Shortbread

Shortbread is a rich and crumbly type of butter biscuit that is traditionally made into wedges but could also be shaped into biscuits or fingers. The high butter content gives shortbread its crumbly or "short" texture. This recipe makes eight wedges.

You will need
155g (5½oz) unsalted butter, softened, plus extra for greasing
75g (2½oz) caster sugar, plus extra for sprinkling
175g (6oz) plain flour
50g (1¾oz) cornflour

1   Lightly grease a 18cm (7in) loose-bottomed, round cake tin and line it with baking parchment.

2   Combine the softened butter and the sugar in a bowl, then cream together using an electric whisk for 2–3 minutes or until very light and fluffy.

3   Sift the flour and cornflour into the bowl and mix. Using your hands, bring the mixture together to form a dough, then place in the tin.

4   Press the dough into the tin using your hands, until it fills the tin and is smooth and even on top. Using a sharp knife, lightly score the shortbread into eight even wedges. Prick the shortbread all over with a fork, then cover it with clingfilm and chill in the fridge for 1 hour.

5   Preheat the oven to 160°C (325°F/Gas 3). Bake the shortbread in the oven for 30–40 minutes, until lightly golden and firm

6   Re-score the wedges using a sharp knife while the shortbread is still warm. Sprinkle a dusting of caster sugar over the top and leave to cool completely. When cool, carefully remove from the tin. Break or cut the shortbread into wedges along the scored lines and serve. The shortbread will keep in an airtight container for five days.

Gingerbread men

These jolly gingerbread men are as much fun to make as they are to receive. Give them raisin faces and buttons or use coloured icing to pipe on facial features, hair, clothes, and accessories. This recipe makes 16 gingerbread men (or ladies).

You will need
4 tbsp golden syrup
300g (10½oz) plain flour, plus extra
        for dusting
1 tsp bicarbonate of soda
1½ tsp ground ginger
1½ tsp mixed spice
100g (3½oz) unsalted butter,
        softened and diced
155g (5½oz) soft, dark brown sugar
1 egg
raisins, to decorate

1 Preheat the oven to 190°C (375°F/ Gas 5). Heat the golden syrup until it liquefies, then cool.

2 Sift the flour, bicarbonate of soda, and spices into a bowl. Add the butter. Rub together with your fingertips until the mixture looks like breadcrumbs. Add the sugar to the mixture and mix well with a wooden spoon.

3 Beat the egg into the cooled syrup with a fork until well blended. Make a well in the flour mixture. Pour in the syrup mix. Bring together to make a rough dough.

4 On a lightly floured work surface, knead the dough briefly until smooth. Flour the dough and the work surface well, and roll the dough out to 5mm (¼in) thick. Using a cutter, cut out as many shapes as possible. Transfer to non-stick baking sheets. Mix the offcuts of dough, re-roll, and cut out more shapes until all the dough is used. Decorate the men with raisins, giving them eyes, a nose, and buttons down the front.

5 Bake for 10–12 minutes until golden. Transfer to a wire rack to cool completely. These gingerbread men will keep in an airtight container for three days.

Spritzgebäck biscuits

These delicate, buttery biscuits are based on a classic German biscuit traditionally served at Christmas. They're a clever twist on traditional butter biscuits, and make an indulgent gift. This recipe makes 45 biscuits.

You will need

380g (13oz) butter, softened
250g (9oz) caster sugar
few drops of vanilla extract
pinch of salt
500g (1lb 2oz) plain flour, sifted
125g (4½oz) ground almonds
2 egg yolks, if needed
100g (3½oz) dark or milk chocolate

Special equipment:
Piping bag and star nozzle

1   Preheat the oven to 180°C (350°F/ Gas 4). Line two or three baking sheets with greaseproof paper. Place the butter in a bowl and beat until smooth. Stir in the sugar, vanilla, and salt until the mixture is thick, and the sugar has been absorbed. Gradually add two-thirds of the flour, stirring in a little at a time.

2   Add the rest of the flour and almonds, and knead the mixture to make a dough. Transfer the dough to a piping bag and squeeze 7.5cm (3in) lengths onto the baking sheets. Loosen the dough with two egg yolks, if necessary.

3   Bake for 12 minutes or until golden, and transfer to a wire rack. Melt the chocolate in a bowl over a pan of simmering water. Dip one end of each biscuit into the melted chocolate and return to the rack to set. The biscuits will keep in an airtight container for two to three days.

Tip: If the dough is too stiff to be piped after adding the eggs, add milk, one tablespoon at a time, until it is loose enough.

Orange crunch biscuits

These crunchy biscuits have been given a tangy twist with orange zest. They can be decorated with orange-flavoured icing for a more intense flavour or made plain for a more subtle taste. This recipe makes 20–24 biscuits.

You will need

125g (4½oz) self-raising flour
60g (2oz) unsalted butter, diced,
        plus extra for greasing
60g (2oz) soft dark brown sugar
½ egg yolk (beaten)
1 tbsp clear runny honey
1 tsp orange zest

For the icing
250g (9oz) icing sugar, sifted
3 tbsp fresh orange juice

Special equipment:
Piping bag and nozzle

1   Sift the flour into a bowl and rub the butter into the flour with your fingertips, until the mixture looks like breadcrumbs. Using a table knife, stir the sugar, orange zest, honey, and egg into the flour and butter, until the mixture starts to come together in lumps.

2   Use your hands to bring the lumps together to form a smooth ball of dough. Briefly knead the dough and then lightly flour the work surface. Roll the dough into a log, about 5cm (2in) in diameter and 10cm (4in) long. Wrap the log in clingfilm and chill it for 1 hour 30 minutes, or until firm.

3   Preheat the oven to 180°C (350°F/ Gas 4). Lightly grease two baking sheets with butter. Slice the log into 20–24 thin discs and place the biscuits on the baking sheets. Bake for 7–9 minutes.

4   Remove the biscuits from the oven and allow to set and cool. Beat the icing sugar and orange juice together to form a smooth paste. Transfer the biscuits to a cooling rack. Put the icing into a piping bag and then drizzle it over the cool biscuits in a zigzag pattern. The biscuits will keep in an airtight container for five to seven days.

Chocolate truffles

Edible gifts

These chocolate truffles look so impressive that you'll be surprised to find how easy they are to make. Coat them with cocoa and icing sugar for a classic look, or with various colourful toppings (see p.181) for a truly tempting box of treats.

To make cocoa- and sugar-coated chocolate truffles you will need

Tools: saucepan • bowl • whisk • teaspoon • tray • greaseproof paper • sieve • plate

Ingredients: 125ml (4fl oz) double cream • 2 tbsp dark rum, brandy, or sherry • 250g (9oz) plain, white, or milk chocolate, melted • 40g (1½oz) cocoa • 20g (¾oz) icing sugar

Makes 30 truffles

1
Place the cream in a saucepan, bring it to the boil to sterilize, then cool until lukewarm. Stir in the rum, brandy, or sherry, then add it to the cool, melted chocolate, stirring until blended.

2
Beat the mixture until light and fluffy, then chill for 2–3 hours until it is firm enough to divide into portions.

179

 3

Using a teaspoon, scoop out balls of the mixture and roll into neat balls. Place them onto a tray lined with greaseproof paper, keeping them well apart. Chill until firm, about one hour.

 4

Sift the cocoa and icing sugar together to create a sugar and cocoa coating.

 5

One at a time, roll the chilled truffles in your hands to soften the outside slightly, then roll them in the cocoa and sugar mixture to coat.

Other coatings

To create a colourful box of truffles, divide the rolled balls into five batches after they have been chilled. Roll each truffle in your hands quickly to soften the outside slightly. Roll the first batch (around six truffles) in 2 tsp cocoa and 1 tsp icing sugar. Roll each of the remaining batches of six in one of the toppings below.

A. 2 tbsp finely chopped pistachio nuts

B. 2 tbsp chocolate vermicelli

C. 2 tbsp dried strawberries, crushed and mixed with icing sugar

D. 2 tbsp finely chopped hazelnuts

Colourful macarons

Light and delicate macarons make a truly sophisticated gift. To make a multi-coloured box, divide up the mixture and add different-coloured food colouring to each batch. These macarons use fresh cream, so keep them chilled.

For pink macarons you will need

Tools: 2 baking sheets • greaseproof paper • 2 large mixing bowls • hand-held electric whisk • piping bag • wire cooling rack • palette knife *Ingredients:* 2 large egg whites at room temperature • 75g (2½oz) granulated sugar • 50g (1¾oz) ground almonds • 100g (3½oz) icing sugar • pink food colouring • 200ml (7fl oz) double cream

Makes 20 macarons

1
Preheat the oven to 150°C (300°F/Gas 2). Line 2 baking sheets with greaseproof paper. Trace 20 x 3cm (1¼in) circles, leaving a good-sized gap between them. Turn the paper over.

2
In a large bowl, whisk the egg whites to stiff peaks using an electric whisk.

3

Add the granulated sugar a little at a time, whisking well between additions. The meringue mixture should be very stiff at this point.

4

Mix together the ground almonds and the icing sugar. Gently fold in the almond mixture, a spoonful at a time, until just incorporated into the meringue mixture.

7

Bake in the middle of the oven for 18–20 minutes, until the surface is set firm. Leave for 15–20 minutes, then transfer to a wire rack to cool completely.

8

Pour the double cream into a bowl, and add some more pink food colouring. Whisk the cream until it is thick and the colour is evenly distributed.

 5
Add a few drops of pink food colouring to the mixture, folding the mixture carefully, until just mixed in.

 6
Transfer the macaron mixture to a piping bag. Using the guidelines, pipe the mixture into the centre of each circle, allowing it to spread and fill out into an even, round shape.

9
Using a palette knife, add a blob of whipped cream to the centre of one macaron half. Add the second half and sandwich gently. Serve immediately.

Creamy fudge

Set up a sweet factory in your kitchen with this quick fudge recipe. Sweet and rich, fudge is delicious plain, but you could try adding nuts, raisins, and chocolate chunks (see p.189) for a variety of tasty treats.

To make creamy fudge you will need

Tools: 18cm (7in) shallow, non-stick square tin • medium heavy-based saucepan • sugar thermometer • wooden spoon • knife **Ingredients:** 450g (1lb) caster sugar • 50g (2oz) unsalted butter, diced • 170ml (6fl oz) can evaporated milk • 150ml (¼ pint) milk • ½ tsp vanilla extract

Makes 36 squares

1 Grease an 18cm (7in) shallow, non-stick square tin.

2 Pour the sugar, butter, and milks into a saucepan.

3

Gently heat the mixture, stirring with
a wooden spoon until all the sugar has
dissolved. Bring to the boil and simmer
continuously for 20–25 minutes.

4

Use a sugar thermometer to monitor the
temperature of the mixture. Once it reaches
116°C (240°F), remove from the heat and
add the vanilla extract.

5

Once off the heat, beat the mixture with
a wooden spoon until it is thick and paler
in colour. Pour it into the prepared tin and
leave it to cool.

6

When cold, lift the fudge from
the tin. Cut it into small squares.

Fudge variations

Create endless variations of the fudge recipe by mixing raisins, chocolate chips, nuts, or even marshmallows into the mixture after it has been thickened in Step 5. Some ideas to get you started are given below.

A. 75g (2½oz) raisins, chopped

B. 155g (5½oz) white chocolate chips

C. 60g (2oz) cashew nuts mixed with 40g (1½oz) raisins

D. 75g (2½oz) pecan nuts, chopped

Flavoured oils

Homemade flavoured oils make beautiful and useful gifts for anyone who loves to cook. Herb-flavoured oils can be used to dress salads or as a base for marinades, while a few drops of chilli oil add zing to pizza and pasta dishes.

To make chilli oil you will need

Tools: knife • chopping board • sterilized glass bottle • jug and funnel (optional)

Ingredients: 1 litre (1¾ pints) light olive oil • 100g (3½oz) mix of red bird's eye chillies and regular red chillies

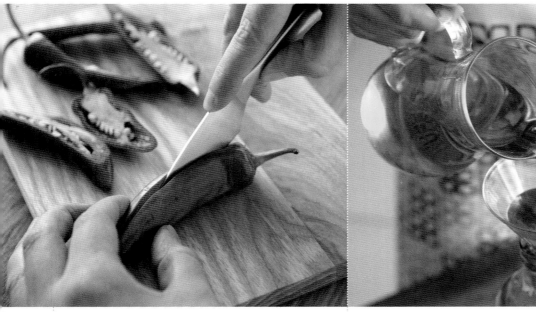

1

Slice the regular chillies in half with a knife, cutting all the way through the stem. Add the sliced chillies, whole bird's eye chillies, and any seeds to the sterilized bottle.

2

Fill up the bottle with 1 litre (1¾ pints) olive oil and stopper it. The oil will keep for up to one month.

Basil oil

Fragrant basil oil makes a flavourful base for salad dressings, and can be used to flavour sauces and soups. Bruising the leaves before you pour on the oil releases their delicate aroma.

You will need
1 litre (1¾ pints) light olive oil
150g (5oz) basil

1 Heat the oil gently in a pan until it reaches 40°C (104°F).

2 Lightly bruise the basil and put it in a warm, sterilized jar or bottle. Pour the warm oil into the jar, then seal. The oil will be ready to use in three to four weeks.

Tip: Filter basil oil after three to four weeks to extend its shelf life. Re-bottle the oil and seal the bottle before storing.

Garlic and rosemary oil

This traditionally flavoured oil can be used as a base for marinades, or to lightly coat vegetables before they are roasted in the oven. The oil keeps for one month.

You will need
6 garlic cloves
3 stalks rosemary
1 litre (1¾ pints) light olive oil

1   Crush the garlic cloves lightly. Place them in a sterilized jar or bottle with the stalks of rosemary.

2   Add oil to the bottle to cover the herbs, then seal.

Tip: Try combining rosemary with herbs such as thyme or coriander for other exciting flavour combinations.

Gift wrap

Square
gift box

Gift wrap

A gift box is the ideal way to present awkwardly shaped gifts. You can make this gift box exactly the required size by re-sizing the template. Use patterned card, or glue decorative paper to card before you start to create different looks.

To make a square gift box you will need

Tools: pencil • scalpel • cutting mat • ruler • blunt knife (or pair of scissors) • rubber
Materials: patterned card (or patterned paper glued onto card) • tracing paper • glue stick

1
Use a photocopier to re-size the box stencil on p.199. Using tracing paper and a pencil, transfer the template onto patterned card (or glue patterned paper to the back of the card).

2
Using a scalpel and a cutting mat, carefully cut out the shape you have drawn. Take care not to cut into the internal folding lines.

3

Once you have cut out the entire shape, score all the folding lines using a ruler and blunt knife, or one side of a pair of scissors. This will make the box easier to assemble.

4

Fold the sides inwards along the scored lines, making sure that each crease is sharp. For a neat finish, rub out the pencil lines along the creases inside the box.

5

Attach the three sides not adjacent to the lid to each other using the glue stick or double-sided sticky tape on the outside of the flaps. Hold in place until set.

6

Fold in the flaps of the last remaining side, spread glue or attach tape to the patterned side of the flaps, and slot the side into place. Press the flaps down, and hold in place until set.

Square gift box template

Please enlarge to the required
size on a photocopier

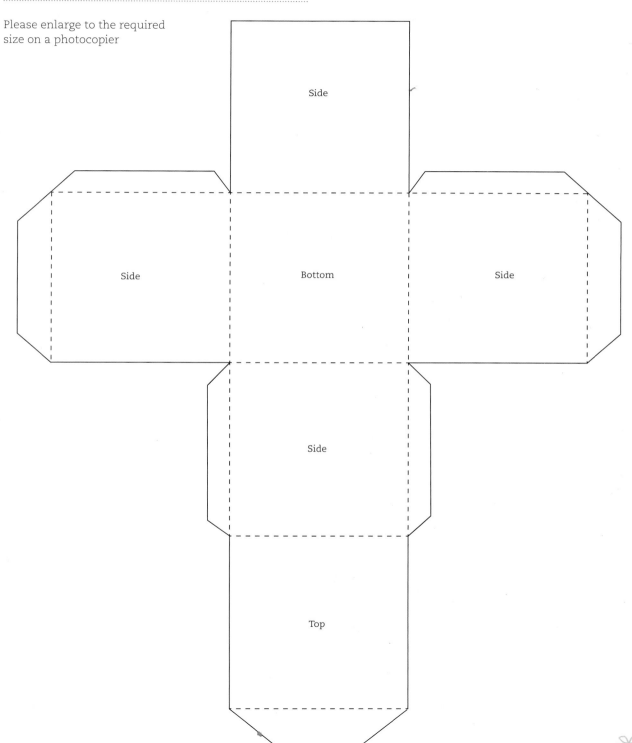

Side

Side

Bottom

Side

Side

Top

Decorating gift boxes

A few odds and ends (coloured paper, ribbons, tissue paper, and buttons) can turn plain wrapped parcels or plain boxes into beautiful, personalized gifts.

A. *Gift tag and ribbon*
Cut a luggage label shape from white card. Punch a hole in the corner and thread through with ribbon. Tie this ribbon around the box and glue the ends at the base of the box. Tie another ribbon in a different colour around the box.

B. *Lots of dots*
Layer sheets of tissue paper in different colours. Cut circles out of the layered sheets of tissue, cutting through all the layers. Using a needle and thread, sew a few small stitches through the centre of each stack of circles to secure and tie off at the back. Glue these to the top.

C. *Button bow*
Cut out four rectangles in two colours of patterned card. Cut a triangle out of one end of each. Glue to the top of the box, layered on top of one another. Cut out a bow-tie shape from patterned card. Fold the sides of the bow-tie shape around and under to meet at the back. Glue this to the box, press down, and glue in the middle to make the 3D bow shape. Glue on a button in the centre of the bow.

D. *Button band*
Cut out a strip of patterned card, long enough to wrap around the box. Sew on a variety of buttons using cream yarn. Wrap the strip around the box and glue at the bottom.

E. *Floral wrap*
Wrap a length of ribbon around the box and glue at the bottom. Cut out and glue another ribbon going the other way. Cut out flower shapes in different colours from tissue paper and layer on top of each other. Sew a few stitches to hold the flowers together. Stick the flowers on the box, where the ribbons meet. Add a few more smaller flowers made using the same method.

F. *Rosette*
Cut two lengths of ribbon and point the ends by cutting out a triangle. Glue these to the top of the box. Using pinking shears, cut circles from patterned card and decorative papers. Cut each circle smaller as you go and stack them up to make the rosette shape. Thread a button through the circles to hold them together then stick on the box.

Tip: All these ideas could be used on larger parcels or boxes. Or why not combine a few?

Jewellery case

This slim case makes the perfect gift box for jewellery and other small items likely to slip out of a looser box. Wrap your gift in tissue paper and close the box with a ribbon tied in a bow to ensure that it stays safe until opened.

To make a jewellery case you will need

Tools: pencil • scalpel • cutting mat • ruler • blunt knife (or pair of scissors) • eraser

Materials: card • tracing paper • tissue paper • glue stick

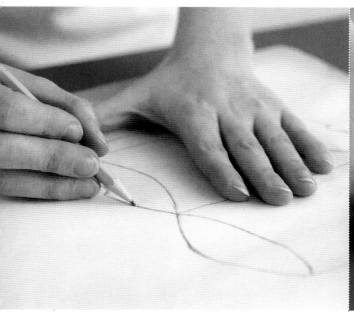

1
Use a photocopier to re-size the template on p.204 if necessary. Transfer it onto a sheet of card using tracing paper and a pencil.

2
Flip the card over. Glue a sheet of tissue paper or decorative paper to the card, ensuring that it is stuck down completely. You could also use patterned card.

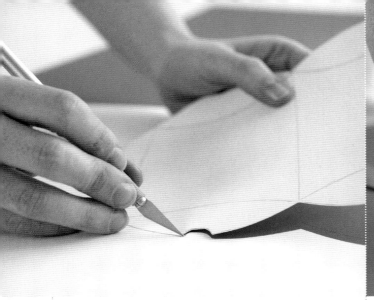

 3

Using a scalpel and a cutting mat, cut around the outside lines of the box. Take care not to cut into the folding lines.

 4

Using a ruler and one side of a pair of scissors, or a blunt knife, score along all the internal folding lines. You can rub out the pencil lines at this point.

 5

Fold the side flap up and spread glue on the patterned side. Fold the case in half and attach the flap to the inside of the opposite edge. Hold it in place until it sticks.

 6

Choose one end to be the bottom of the case. Fold in the first flap along the curved line, and then the other. Fill the box and fold in the flaps at the other end to close.

Jewellery case template

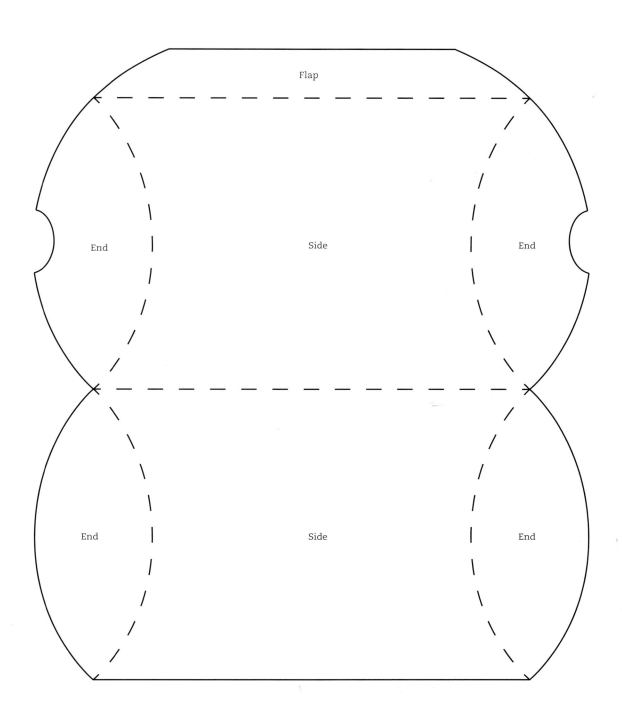

Flap

End

Side

End

End

Side

End

Pyramid boxes

Gift wrap

These small boxes are quick and easy to make, requiring no gluing at all. They are the ideal size for a small gift, or to hold sweets or party favours. Personalize your boxes by using different colours and types of ribbon.

To make a pyramid box you will need

Tools: pencil • scalpel • cutting mat • blunt knife (or pair of scissors) • eraser • hole punch

Materials: patterned card (or patterned paper glued onto card) • tracing paper • ribbon

1

Use a photocopier to re-size the template on p.209, if required. Using tracing paper and a pencil, transfer it onto a sheet of patterned card (or glue decorative paper to the card).

2

Using a scalpel and a cutting mat, cut around the outside of the box template. Take care not to cut into the internal folding lines.

3

Lightly score along the fold lines using a ruler and a blunt knife (or one side of a pair of scissors).

4

Add a hole to the tip of each triangle using a hole punch. Try to keep them evenly spaced and ensure they are not too close to the edges in any direction.

5

For a neat finish, rub out the fold lines. Fold each section and flap along the scored lines, ensuring that each crease is sharp.

6

Assemble the pyramid box by folding in each side and tucking each flap into the centre of the box. Fasten the box by threading a ribbon through the holes and tying a knot or bow.

Pyramid box template

Please enlarge to the required
size on a photocopier

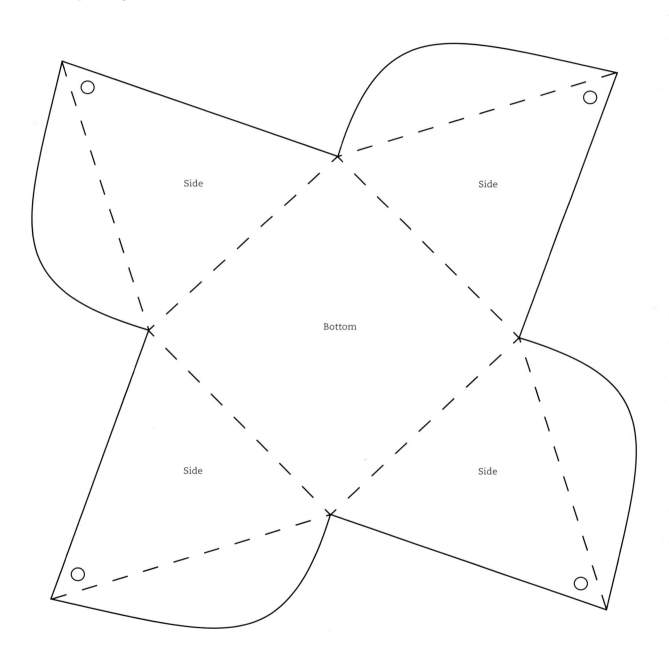

Side

Side

Bottom

Side

Side

Homemade
gift bags

Gift wrap

Follow this simple tutorial to turn any sheet of wrapping paper or gift wrap into a bespoke gift bag. For an even more personalized bag, use a sheet of paper printed with a message, or even a printout of a photograph.

To make a gift bag you will need

Tools: pencil • scissors • blunt knife (or pair of scissors) • glue stick • hole punch

Materials: tracing paper • wrapping paper or other printed or plain paper • card • ribbon

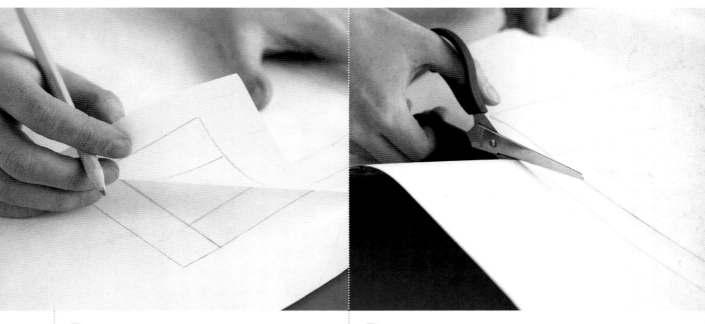

1

Re-size the template from pp.214–215 to the required size on a photocopier. Using tracing paper and a pencil, transfer the template onto the wrong side of your chosen paper.

2

Cut out the bag shape along the outer lines. Take care to not cut along any of the internal folding lines.

211

3

Score along the horizontal top and bottom folding lines, using a ruler and a blunt knife (or one side of a pair of scissors). Fold down the bottom and top flaps, making sure the creases are sharp.

4

Score along each of the vertical folding lines, going across the top and bottom flaps. Then fold the bag in along each of these lines in turn, again making sharp creases.

7

Fold the bottom of the bag as if you were wrapping a present. Fold one long side of the bottom tab in across the opening, creasing the sides sharply. Fold the sides in over the opening, again creasing sharply. Finally, fold in the remaining side to cover the opening, and glue or tape the base down.

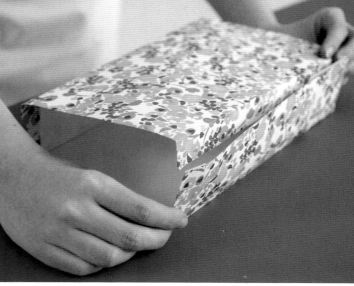

5

Using a glue stick, spread glue evenly along the top flap. Smooth it down, holding it in place until it sticks. This will help the bag hold its shape.

6

Fold out the bottom flap. Spread glue along the outside of the side tab, and attach it to the inside of the opposite end, all the way along its length. Glue the other side tab over the seam.

8

Cut out a piece of card the size of the base of the bag, and place it in the bottom of the bag. This will strengthen the base.

9

Using a two-hole punch (or a single-hole punch), punch two holes on each long side of the bag, through the centre of the reinforced top fold. Add ribbon for handles.

Gift bag template

Top

JOIN

Bottom

JOIN

Side
tab

215

Twist-top gift box

This ingenious gift box comes complete with its own closing mechanism – specially shaped flaps twist and lock together to hide your surprise inside. Perfect for wrapping up homemade sweets or jewellery in style.

To make a twist-top gift box you will need

Tools: pencil • scalpel • cutting mat • ruler • blunt knife (or pair of scissors)
Materials: card • tracing paper • decorative paper or wrapping paper • glue stick

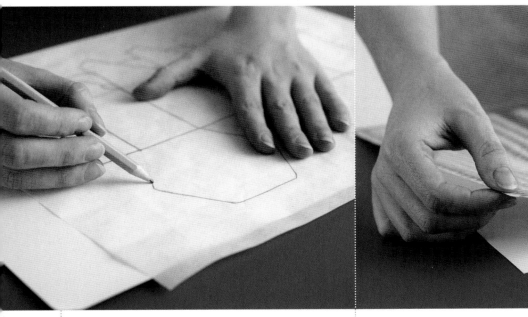

1
Use a photocopier to re-size the twist-top box template on pp.220–221, if required. Use tracing paper and a pencil to transfer the pattern onto a sheet of card.

2
Glue a sheet of wrapping paper or decorative paper to the reverse of the card. Alternatively, you could use patterned card to make the box.

3

Using a scalpel and cutting mat, carefully cut around the pattern. First cut along the outermost lines of the template.

4

Next, using the template on pp.220–221 as a guide, cut into the shape along the lines marked as cutting lines. Finally, remove the small shapes in the top as marked.

6

Fold all the scored lines as marked, ensuring that all the creases are sharp. Assemble the body of the box by gluing both side flaps to the opposite side of the box.

5

Using a ruler and a blunt knife (or one side of a pair of scissors) score all the dashed lines from the wrong side of the card. Score the lines marked with dashes and dots from the right side of the card.

7

Assemble the base of the box by first folding in the piece marked Base 1. Next fold down the two base flaps, and finally Base 2, tucking the attached flaps into the box.

8

Ensure that each of the creases made to the top part of the box is creased in the correct direction. Fill the box and push the flaps down and towards the centre to seal it.

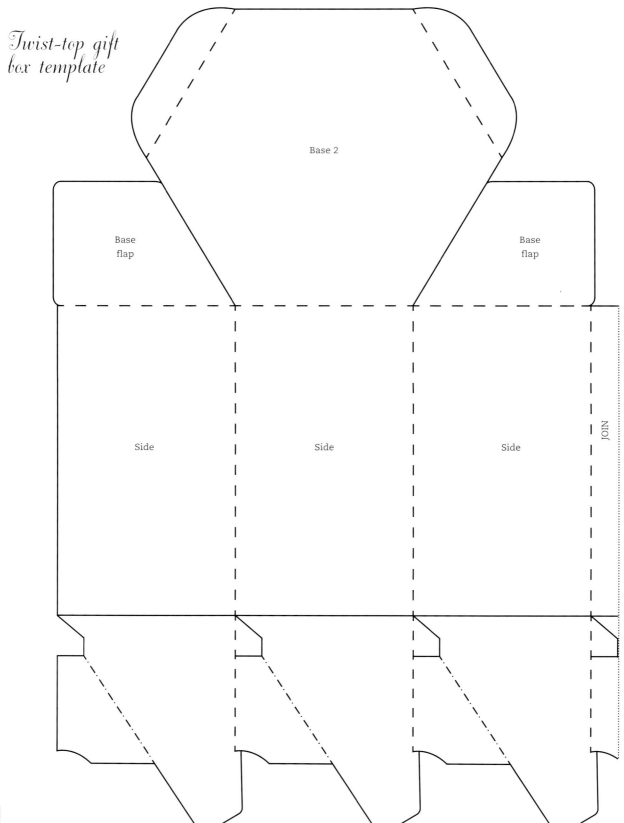

Twist-top gift
box template

Base 2

Base
flap

Base
flap

Side

Side

Side

JOIN

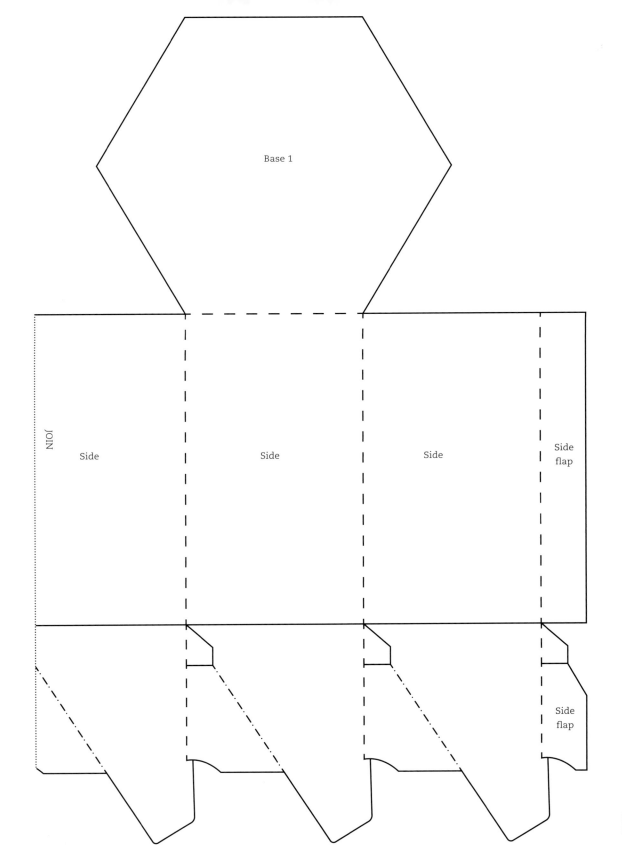

Base 1

JOIN

Side

Side

Side

Side
flap

Side
flap

221

Printed
gift wrap

Gift wrap

Making your own gift wrap finishes off any gift with a personal touch. This stamped pattern of blocks of stripes is easy to create. Once you have mastered this technique, why not try creating your own shapes and patterns?

To make printed gift wrap you will need

Tools: scissors • glue

Materials: wood or balsa wood block • foam board • inkpad • sheets of white paper

1

To make a line stamp, start with a wooden block. Cut out strips of the desired width from foam board. Glue the strips to one side of a block and allow the glue to dry.

2

To make line-printed gift wrap, press the stamp on an inkpad and stamp in one corner of a sheet of paper. Continue stamping the paper, alternating the orientation of the stamp, until the paper is filled.

223

Templates

Blossom cushion (pp.14-17)

Please enlarge to the required size on a photocopier

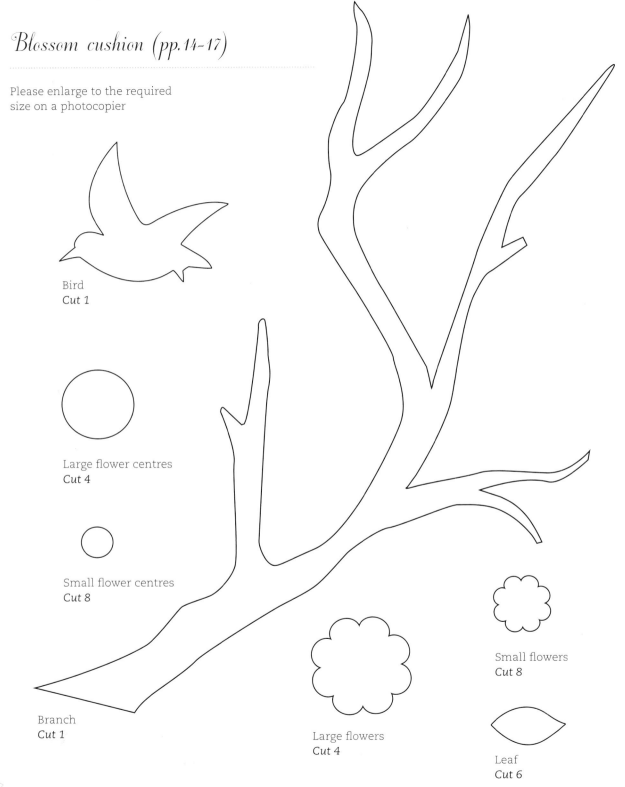

Bird
Cut 1

Large flower centres
Cut 4

Small flower centres
Cut 8

Branch
Cut 1

Large flowers
Cut 4

Small flowers
Cut 8

Leaf
Cut 6

Skull and crossbones cushion (p. 19)

Please enlarge to the required
size on a photocopier

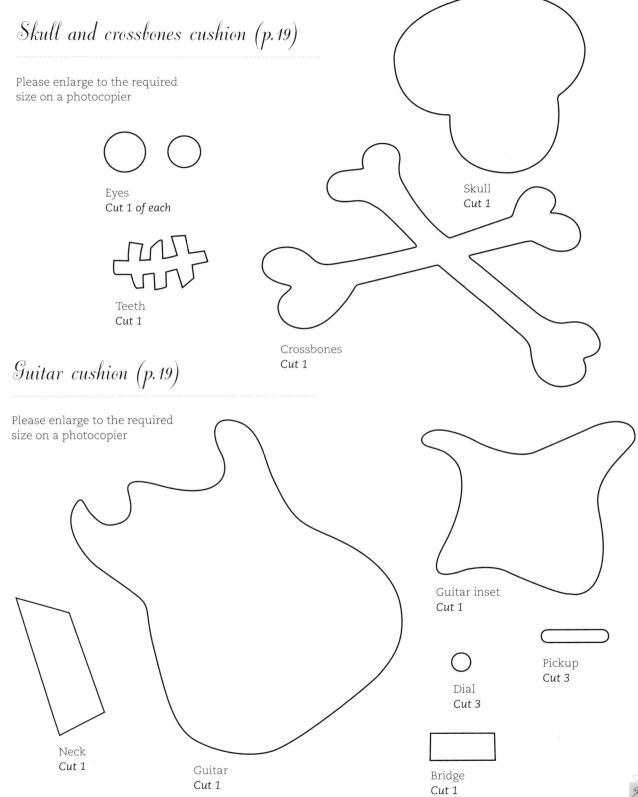

Eyes
Cut 1 of each

Teeth
Cut 1

Skull
Cut 1

Crossbones
Cut 1

Guitar cushion (p. 19)

Please enlarge to the required
size on a photocopier

Guitar inset
Cut 1

Dial
Cut 3

Pickup
Cut 3

Neck
Cut 1

Guitar
Cut 1

Bridge
Cut 1

Castle cushion (p.18)

Please enlarge to the required
size on a photocopier

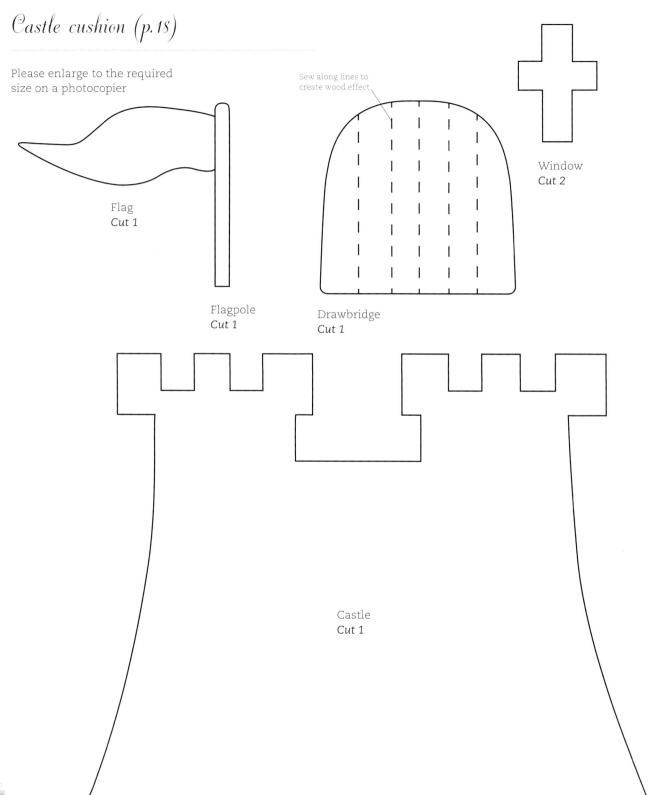

Flag
Cut 1

Flagpole
Cut 1

Sew along lines to
create wood effect

Drawbridge
Cut 1

Window
Cut 2

Castle
Cut 1

Castle cushion dolls (p.18)

Please enlarge to the required
size on a photocopier

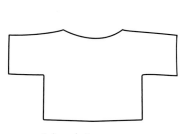

Prince's top
Cut 2
*If making the clothes out of felt, place pieces around doll and
sew together from the outside. If using other fabric, add a seam
allowance, sew together with right sides facing, and turn.*

Princess's dress
Cut 2

Body
Cut 2 for each doll.
*Sew together along
the edges, leaving a
gap. Turn, stuff, and
sew the gap closed.*

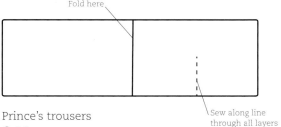

Fold here

Sew along line
through all layers
to make legs

Prince's trousers
Cut 1
Wrap around doll and sew in place.

Crown
*Wrap around head
and sew in place.*

Rollaway gameboard (pp.46–51)

Type of fabric	Cut	Measurements in cm and in
Board: dark fabric	x 5	5 x 40cm (2 x 16in)
Board: light fabric	x 5	5 x 40cm (2 x 16in)
Outer fabric	x 1	30 x 50cm (12 x 20in)
Inner fabric	x 2	30 x 14cm (12 x 5¾in)
Inner fabric	x 2	5 x 27cm (2 x 10¾in)
Interfacing	x 1	30 x 50cm (12 x 20in)
Interfacing	x 1	30 x 14cm (12 x 5¾in)

Appliqué pet portrait (pp.159-161)

Please enlarge to the required size on a photocopier

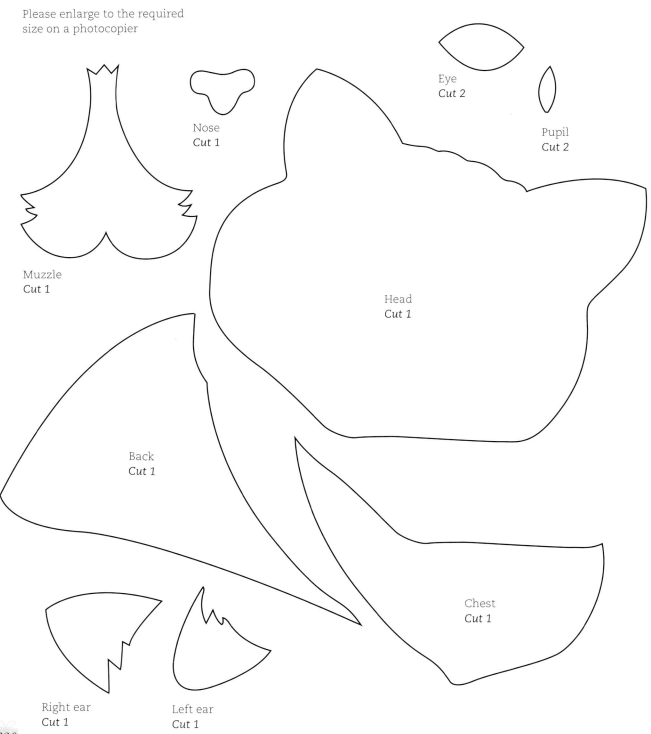

Nose
Cut 1

Eye
Cut 2

Pupil
Cut 2

Muzzle
Cut 1

Head
Cut 1

Back
Cut 1

Chest
Cut 1

Right ear
Cut 1

Left ear
Cut 1

Simple silhouette pet portrait (p. 158)

Please enlarge to the required
size on a photocopier

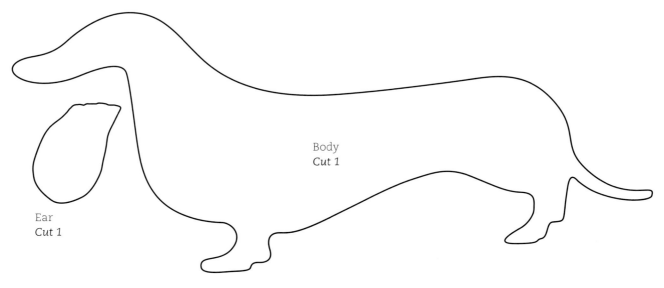

Body
Cut 1

Ear
Cut 1

Catnip mice (pp. 150–153)

Please enlarge to the required
size on a photocopier

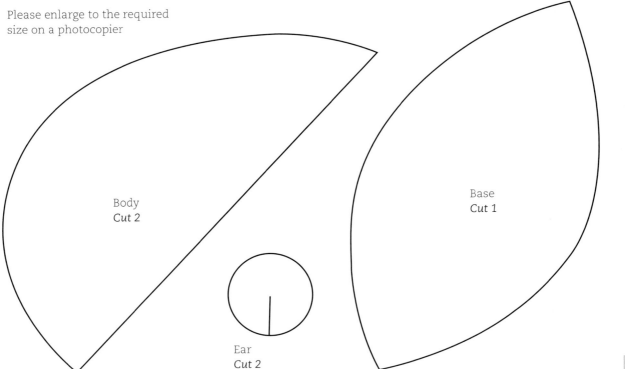

Body
Cut 2

Base
Cut 1

Ear
Cut 2

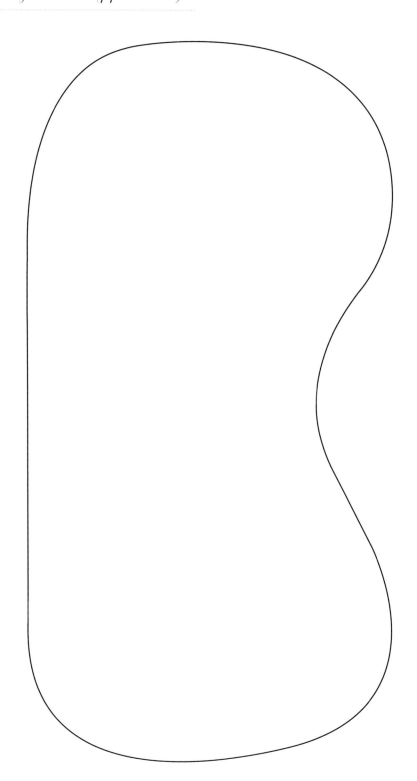

Cat's playmat (pp. 146-149)

Please enlarge to the required
size on a photocopier

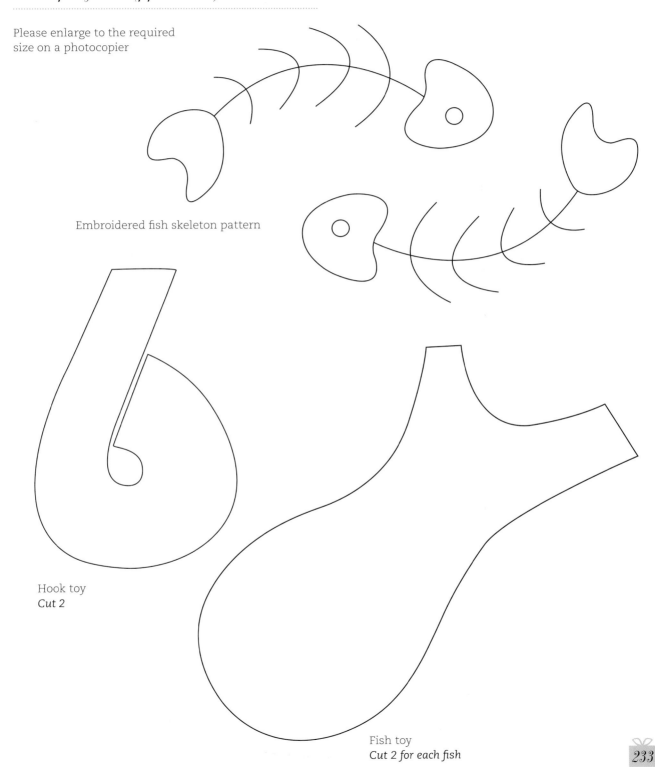

Embroidered fish skeleton pattern

Hook toy
Cut 2

Fish toy
Cut 2 for each fish

Tartan dog jacket (pp. 162-165)

Please enlarge to the required
size on a photocopier

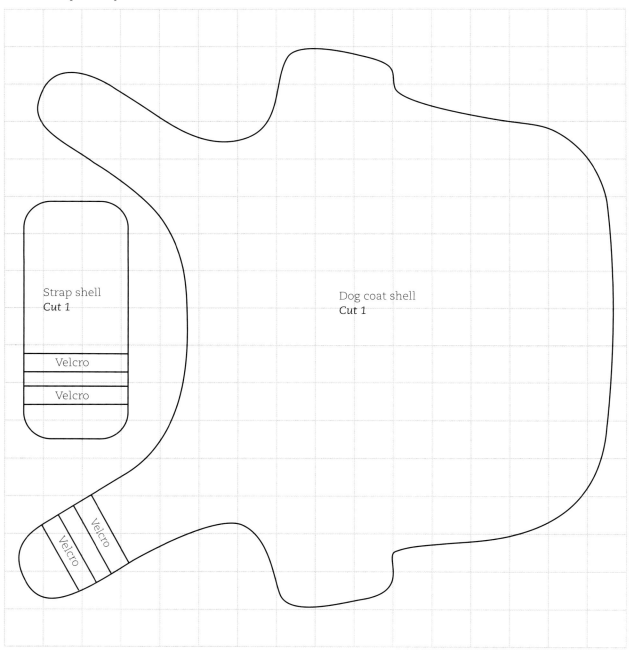

Strap shell
Cut 1

Dog coat shell
Cut 1

Velcro

Velcro

Velcro

Velcro

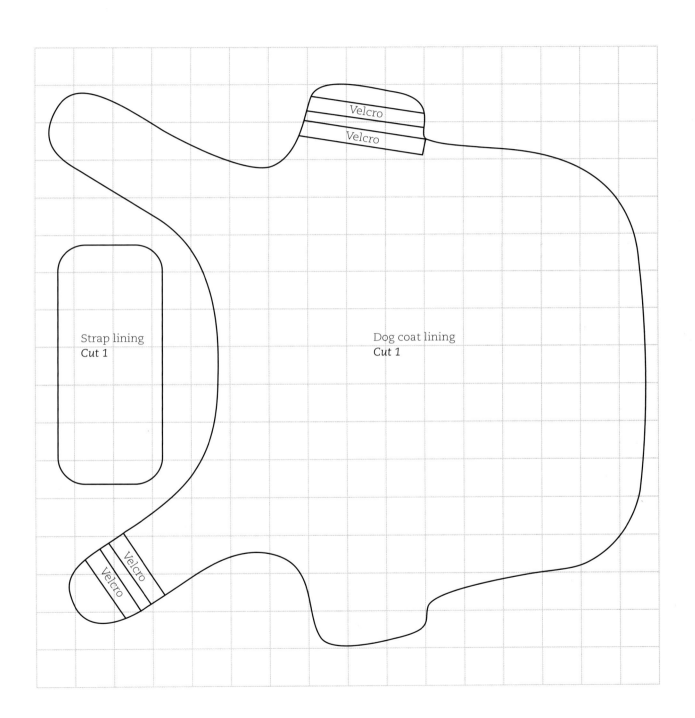

Velcro
Velcro

Strap lining
Cut 1

Dog coat lining
Cut 1

Velcro
Velcro

Ribbon-bound photo album (pp.38-43)

Please enlarge to the required
size on a photocopier

Hole 1

Hole 2

Hole 3

Hole 4

Hole 5

Hole 6

Silver clay jewellery (pp.64-69)

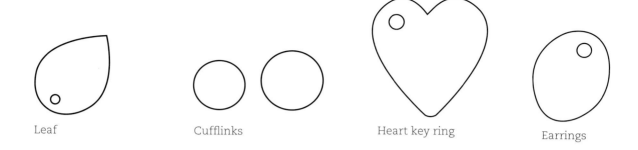

Leaf

Cufflinks

Heart key ring

Earrings

Embellished felt brooches (pp.60-63)

Wing

Bird

Heart

Face

Belly

Wing

Owl

Paisley

Mosaic seaside coasters (p.37)

Mosaic owl jewellery box (p.36)

Top of box

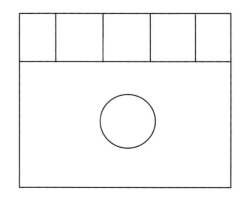

Side of box

Mosaic flower garland mirror (p.36)

Mosaic round tealight holder (p.37)

Please enlarge to the required
size on a photocopier

Dot-decorated mug and coaster set (p.30)

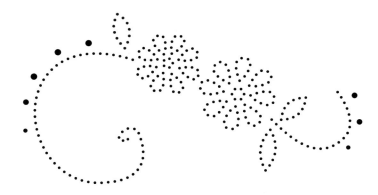

Dot-decorated bunting plate (p.31)

Please enlarge to the required
size on a photocopier

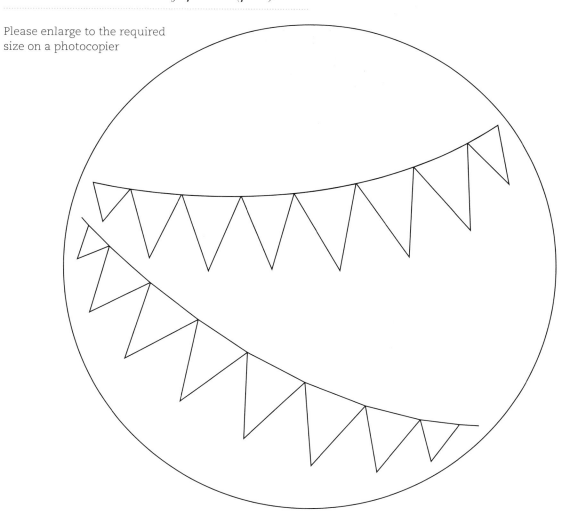

Stencilled bags (pp.84–89)

Please enlarge to the required
size on a photocopier

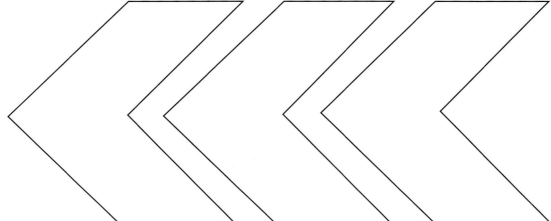

Stitched bag

Pencil illusion

Repeated chevrons

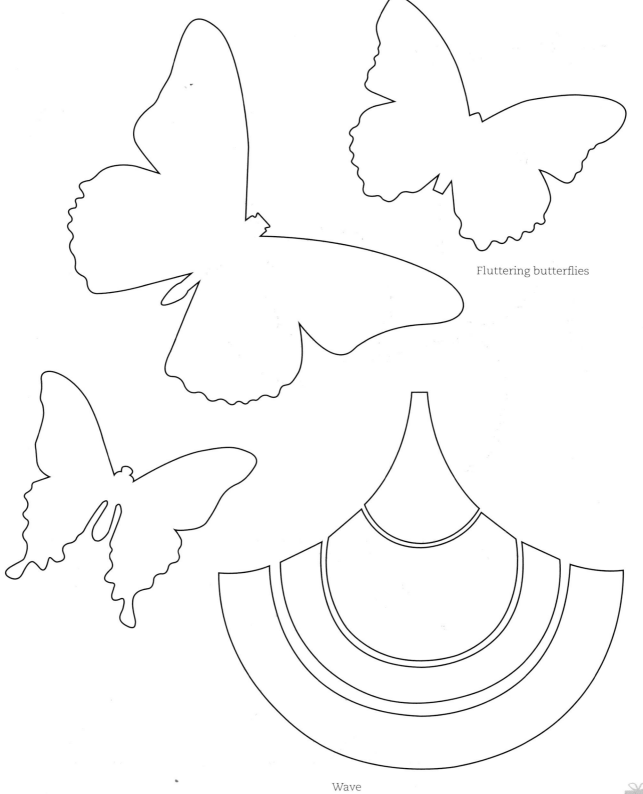

Fluttering butterflies

Wave

Crochet basics

Use this quick-reference guide to (re)familiarize yourself with four basic crochet stitches. These are adapted slightly to make the crochet projects in this book.

Chain stitch (ch)

1 Make a slip knot. Hold the slip knot firmly between finger and thumb.

2 Wrap the yarn over the hook (called "yarn over" or "yo") and catch it with the hook.

3 Pull the hook and yarn back through the stitch.

4 The chain stitch is complete. Repeat steps 2–4 to continue the chain. Count the "V" shapes to count the chains.

Double crochet (dc)

1 To make a row of double crochet, first work 1 ch. Push the hook into the centre of the second stitch from the hook.

2 Wrap the yarn over the hook (yo).

3 Hook the yarn and pull through the first loop.

4 Bring the hook out. There are now two loops on the hook.

5 Wrap the yarn over the hook (yo). Hook the yarn and pull through both loops.

6 Now one loop is left on the hook. The double crochet stitch is complete. Repeat steps 1–5 to make the next stitch, and continue until the end of the row.

Half treble crochet (htr)

1 To make a row of half treble crochet, first work 2 ch. Wrap the yarn over the hook (yo).

2 Push the hook through the centre "V" of the next stitch.

3 Wrap the yarn over the hook again.

4 Pull the yarn through the first loop. There are now three loops on the hook.

5 Wrap the yarn over the hook. Hook the yarn and pull it through all three loops.

6 Now one loop is left on the hook. This completes the half treble stitch. Repeat steps 1–5 to make more half trebles.

Slip stitch (ss)

With one loop on the hook, hook into the next stitch, catch the yarn and pull the loop through the stitch and loop in one movement.

Pull the yarn through

One stitch left on the hook

Index

Acknowledgments

Dorling Kindersley would like to thank Kate Blinman for testing the recipes and for her assistance on the photo shoot; Ruth Jenkinson for additional photography; Becky Alexander, Christine Stroyan, and Katharine Goddard for editorial assistance; Angela Baynham for sense-checking; Katie Hardwicke for proofreading; and Marie Lorimer for indexing.

The authors

A skilled and dedicated team of crafters contributed their time and expertise towards the making of this book. We hope you've been inspired by their talent and creativity.

Hannah Moore

Rollaway gameboard

Catnip mice

Appliqué pet portrait

Appliqué silhouette

Cat's playmat

Customized cushion

Guitar cushion

Skull and crossbones cushion

Castle cushion

Caroline Stamps

Sweet dreams eye mask

Oilcloth wash bag

Kathryn Johnson

Embellished felt brooches

Isabel de Cordova

Travel candle

Layered candle

Candles in ramekins

Three-wick candle

The Oxford Soap Company

All-natural luxury soaps

Moulded vanilla stars

See-through orange soap

Cookie-cutter lavender hearts

Juniper cake-slice soap

Fizzy bath bombs

Ria Holland

Dot-decorated ceramics

Celebration bunting plate

Mug and coaster set

Paula Keogh

Manicure roll

Tartan dog jacket

Kate Davis

Silk scarf

Nicola Barter

Wave-patterned bag

Stitched bag

Pencil illusion bag

Repeated chevrons bag

Fluttering butterflies bag

Clara Smith

Silver leaf pendant

Simple button cufflinks

Leaf bracelet

Wallpaper earrings

Lace heart key ring

Gemma Fletcher

Dog biscuits

Knotted scarf

Colour-block scarf

Close-weave scarf

Beaded necklace

Button-bead necklace

Glass-bead necklace

Painted beads

Victoria Read

Personlized journal

Ribbon-bound photo album

Portrait photo album

Glenda Fisher

Crochet flowers

Belinda Nicholson

Découpage bangle

Claire Montgomerie

Crochet necklace

Lova Rajaonarimanana

Phone and tablet protectors

Karen Mitchell

Mosaic bowl

Flower garland mirror

Seaside coasters

Round tealight holder

Owl jewellery box

Charlotte Johnson

Pyramid boxes

Jewellery case

Homemade gift bags

Square gift box

Twist-top gift box

Carol Doherty

Clasp-frame bag

Clasp-frame purse

Clasp-frame make-up bag

Helen Fickling

Teacup candle